Bits and Pieces

Michael Mc Cone

*Aunt Edna,
Mom thinks I'm famous enough to be autographing books.
Michael McCone*

All rights reserved
© 2011 by Michael Mc Cone
Cover Art Michael Mc Cone
This book, or parts thereof, may not be
reproduced in any form without permission.
Michael_mccone@hotmail.com

ISBN: 978-1-257-44017-7

Dedication

This could be long, so I'll use a really small font.

<small>To my father who taught me to love and to think and to respect. He taught me to be the man I am. To my mother who gushes over everything I do and begged me to promise that I would never stop writing. To my genius brothers, nyeh-nyeh nyeh nyeh nyeh. I published something before you. Thanks for believing I could. To John and Shannon. You guys rock. Hey John, I typed this on the computer you built. To Mrs. West, your Friday writer's workshop days lit this fuse. To Carol Georgi, Ray Zepeda, Brian Lane, Casey Case, and Mike Edwards, the teachers who inspired me to write. Cody Gratner for sharing his sense of humor. To the sunny days that I would go skate to work out my writer's block, and to the dreams that gave me ideas. To God, my creator, but I don't want it to be that trite kind of afterthought dedication. You made me as You saw fit. I hope this pleases You.</small>

> When I run, I run to win. I will never jog, but I will go for a stroll.
> —Eric Liddell

Table of Contents

Fairy Tale Cover Letter 1
The Recipe 3
Who I Am 5
Assertive Cover Letter 7
Creataholic 9
Medical Ad Cover Letter 11
Gladiator 13
10 Reasons Cover Letter 15
Bus Stop 17
Mountain Top 21
A Surfer's Christmas 25
Script Format 27
PSA 29
Car Commercial 31
That Look 33
Soap Commercial 35
The Devil and the Salesman 37
Interrogation 41
Hades Sent 47
Code Name: Traveler 53
The Day After Christmas 61
PB&J 63
May First 65
Escort 75
Solitude 83
Beautiful Art Brutal Craft 95
The Limit 105
A Dollar Short 171
Wedding Speech 223
My Father's Funeral 225
Bits and Pieces 229

This is a compilation of stuff: short stories, scripts, skits, a poem – yes, just one poem – and all kinds of other writing that I have done over the years. Some of it is from school assignments and other bits of it are just because I felt like writing whatever at the time.

Terms of Use

"The Devil and the Salesman" and "A Dollar Short" may be used for a production as long as I am credited as the writer. The short stories may be used in a church service or other ministry avenue, although please, I beg of you, don't paraphrase. Many a wonderful story has been stripped of its impact by paraphrase. Read it in its entirety, set the mood with the right music and lighting. In short don't waste the opportunity of a willing audience.

It was always my dream to make my living by being creative. Writing for a video game studio or advertising agency was my El Dorado. These are the cover letters that I used to try and snag the attention of prospective employers.

The bracketed place holders are to protect the anonymity of entities that will remain anonymous.

The Fairy Tale Cover Letter

To Whom It May Concern:

Okay, here's what happened. Just the other day Bigfoot and I were talking about how much I would love to be a narrative designer for [Generic Company Name]. He encouraged me to go for it so I sat down to write a cover letter. I had just tapped out the first few key strokes when the Easter Bunny tumbled through my door and was tackled by Dracula. While playing Monopoly, bunny boy had been sneaking money from the bank, Drac accused him of cheating, the Easter Bunny told him to go suck an egg and a chase had ensued. I sent the Easter Bunny to go play with his Peeps and got Dracula to go hang with the Chupacabra.

Resuming my letter I got a full three sentences written, three really good, nigh perfect sentences, when Cinderella burst in weeping and wailing that her life was over. She always comes to me with boyfriend drama. Captain Nemo had missed their dinner date. When Ella slipped over to his place to see if he was all right she happened to catch the Tooth Fairy slipping more than a quarter under Captain Nemo's pillow. What could I say? I had told her he was a pirate, but she was sure she could have some fairy-tale romance. I told her to go stay with her step-mother for a few days and she'd have a new perspective.

After ushering Ella out, I locked the door so that I wouldn't be interrupted. Without warning my computer died. Three blind mice had found their way behind the tower and tripped over the power cord. When I got the computer powered back up I realized I hadn't saved my work. An entire evening's effort, shot. And, with those perfect sentences, too.

Of course, I was wondering if anything else could go wrong when the phone rang. It was the Boogie Man. He was having a party at his house. Medusa had gotten stoned out of her mind, Bloody Mary had had one too many and locked herself in the bathroom, Peter Pan was high on fairy dust, and the designated driver, Rip Van Winkle, was zonked on the couch. It was up to me to save the day. By the time I got everyone safely home I had forgotten everything I meant to put in my cover letter. I asked my Fairy Godmother what I should do and she said she had already sent you my cover letter. I don't know what she sent you. I hope this explains the situation sufficiently.

                                        Your Humble
                                        Servant,

                                        Knight in Shining
                                        Armor

I don't believe that I ever submitted the recipe to any prospective employers. It sat unfinished while I was doing my main job hunting and I finished it on principle. It just didn't have the punch that the other had, but I liked it because it was different from the norm and different from what I had done before.

The Recipe

Aunt Jemima's All-Purpose Excellent Copy Writer

Ingedients:
9 - Childhood years soaked in the imaginary kingdoms and adventures of a vacant field.
3 - Adolescent years spent folding Origami and neglecting homework.
7 - Teenage years buried in every Fantasy and Sci-Fi book at hand.
1 - Relationship with mother. (strained)
1 - Unconditionally loving father.
2 - Genius brothers.
1 - Near fatal snowboarding accident. (shredded)
3 - Incredibly stupid stunts.
A handful of road trips of varying length.
A dash of girlfriend drama.

In a large bowl mix all the years, relationships with mother and father, and the brothers until well blended. Let rise in The Valley of the Sickness for 16 years. Knead in the Snowboarding accident until tough.

In a separate container mix the stupid stunts, girlfriend drama, and road trips. It's ok to leave lumps, it adds character.

In a large pan alternate layers of the two mixtures. Pound in a generous amount of Martial arts training. Bake in Long Beach for 2 to 2½ years. While cooling, glaze with hours upon hours of surfing. Best if served hot with pink lemonade.

The next one was a little more serious than some of the other cover letters. I was going for a balance of creativity that didn't veer too far from the mainland.

Who I Am Cover Letter

To Whom It May Concern:

Who am I? I am the sum of coffee grounds and ice cream, fourth grade gymnastics and college martial arts, before-dawn surfing and after-dark billiards, Netherlandic black metal and Hans Zimmer movie scores. I am a product of the K-12 system, community and state college, and every curve that life has thrown at me. My mother tells me I am wonderful, my father tells me I am a joy, my students tell me I am the coolest teacher ever, my friends tell me I am things that I will not repeat in polite company. My doctor tells me I'm healthy, my brother tells me I'm sick, and my MMA instructor tells me I'm a nut. A conglomeration of comedy and drama, love and loss, insight and inquiry is who I am.

I am a twenty-six-solar-year-aged, carbon-based life form from the third planet of a solar system located in the Orion arm of the Milky Way Galaxy. I am a resident of O-Town, born in Bishop and quickened in Long Beach. I am a zealous worker when required, a sitcomian slacker when allowed, a caring, if bony, shoulder to cry on when needed, and a smile when you least expect it.

I am at peace in the ocean, on the soccer field, and on the road. I am at war with mediocrity and the status quo, intent on changing the world. I am a wonderer, a dreamer, a genius. I am the physical housing of the finest imagination money can't buy. I am a wellspring of ideas and a vault of experience. I am all this and yet every day I discover myself again. I am a full circle that continues to grow.

I am interested in utilizing my creative talents and education to add to what [company name] already offers its clients and in turn having my own creativity pushed to a new level. I thank you for your time and look forward to hearing from you.

                                        Respectfully yours,

This was the cover letter that started all the others. I had been doing the same boring, here's my education, here's my experience letter that everyone does. But I was applying for positions where the goal was to be creative. So, I went for it.

The Assertive Cover Letter

To Whom It May Concern:

What qualifies me to be part of [company's name] creative team? Only the finest imagination money can't buy. Countless evenings spent in the field behind my house, shirking homework with my brothers, imagining we were heroes upon an arduous task of epic scale, thousands of hours spent ignoring my high school teachers so I could finish devouring the next chapter of Terry Brooks' newest book, games of Magic The Gathering that ended only because the sun rose far too early the next morning, and innumerable sleep-deprived nights with friends where I was not mild mannered Michael Mc Cone, but Kellenkan Roaminghand, the thief whose skills and wit managed to deliver his companions from the dire trouble he most likely got them into in the first place, have cultivated an imagination of dynastic scope.

If we must consult this dismally mundane world for my exploits their broad range will not fail to impress upon you my fitness to create for [company name]. From an internship with the people that brought the world Bay Watch to teaching grade school, from surfing before sunrise to serving Starbucks coffee until after midnight, from meetings with writers and producers at the Disney Channel to creating a fictitious band and recording music for them the weekend I should have been studying for finals, and from hiding second-degree burned legs to attending martial arts class with a torn spleen, there is so much experience jammed into this skull that even I begin to think I'm lying about it. Every scrap of experience is cannibalized to nourish creativity.

7

I don't just write; I vomit content. It's good, it's bad, it's brilliant, and there is always more of it. All of it filled with Germanisms, enallages (not to be confused with analogies), locutions, memes, tropes, and neologisms, each more you-must-have-sold-your-soul-to-Satan-to-craft-that, brilliant than the last. You need an innovative way to say "our company kills bugs real good," I'm on it. The phrase that refuses to allow you to ignore it, I'll get it. All this and so much more pulse through my cerebellum. And that's without any coffee. That is why I am, irrefragably, unambiguously, and incomprehensibly qualified to be one of [company position].

                    Respectfully
                    yours

    My friend Cody could not believe that I had really sent this out as a cover letter. I figured that showing a prospective boss that I was creative was a lot better than telling them that I was creative. I received a letter from the CEO of the company that I had sent it to. They weren't looking for anyone, but he thanked me for doing something that was not the average, boring cover letter.

I thought it would be an interesting turn to have the positive things from a cover letter presented as a negative in spoof. Its weakness is that it fails to state what position I am going for. It would be kind of hard to say that I am going for a copy writing position since I am presenting writing as if it were a bad thing.

There is no sign off for this letter either. It didn't seem to be fitting. I figured I could get away with it as well since the last line restates my name.

The Creataholic Cover Letter

To Whom It May Concern:

My name is Michael McCone, and I am ashamed to say that for the last ten years I have been… a writer. Bibliophage, word junky, text fiend, yes, I have been them all. If you would have confronted me about it even a week ago, I would have denied it. For so long I was in denial. For years the slightest insinuation that I was using performance enhancing adverbs would have been vehemently refuted. But, I can't hide any more.

I started out light, at first. A little description now and then, some dialogue to unwind after a hard day's work. I tried to ignore the vocabularian track marks forming. I thought I had a grip on it. What could be the harm in dropping a pun here or there? Then, one morning, I realized that I was no longer reading other's chapters. I was writing my own.

I threw away my pens and notebooks, but it was a futile gesture. I found myself writing on napkins, receipts, and even the backs of business cards. I was borrowing pens to jot down ideas; I couldn't stop. The light hit me one morning as I was about to write on the bulletin at church. At church! That's when I knew I needed professional help. That's why I've come to you. I am Michael Mc Cone, and I am a creataholic.

9

Medical ads are great. They are often really funny, especially when they are not trying to be. They are so sing-song and pleasant sounding, even when naming side effects that are at times worse than the problem they are treating.

The Medical Ad Cover Letter

To Whom It May Concern:

Do you or a loved one suffer from bland correspondence, lack of adjectival variety, using the same cliché time after time, or flat, lifeless text? Have you ever thought it was just the topic that was inherently boring? These symptoms may be part of a larger problem. You may be suffering from Creatile Dysfunction. CD affects millions of Americans each year and if left untreated may become a serious health risk for those in the creative field. Thankfully, CD is easily treatable. The answer is here.

Introducing Michael, the first and only, non-habit forming, creative aid. Michael is an all-natural cure for your creative needs. Side effects are generally mild and include increased smiling, spikes in physical activity, random acts of kindness, and in some cases, napping. In rare instances those taking Michael have been know to step outside their comfort zone and try something completely new.

Check with your doctor to see if you are healthy enough to start a creative project before you begin taking a creative aid. Michael is right for everyone. It is safe to take Michael if you are, or plan on becoming, pregnant. If at any time while you are taking Michael you experience giddiness, exuberance, or flat out joy, do not be alarmed; Michael is working. Michael does not interact with any other medications. Go ahead and take Michael if you are taking nitrates for chest pain. Don't let CD ruin your life. Now is the time to generate creativity the all-natural way, and start living the life you deserve.

I don't believe I ever sent this one off. It wasn't developed enough. I love the fact that it doesn't have, nor does it need, the normally expected salutation. It's a bit risky if the person hasn't seen Gladiator or doesn't remember the scene where the gladiators shout to Caesar, but the payoff is worth it in my eyes.

The Gladiator Cover Letter

We, who are about to apply, salute you!

I enter this arena armed to the teeth with experience, creativity, and self-expectation. My armor, will and wit. Does any other applicant wish to contest me?

I have faced the unforgiving hordes of elementary school children and brought them to heel. I have survived time with a Hollywood studio and come out all the stronger for it. I have served time in the Starbucks fleet, chained to the espresso machines, but they could not break me.

Now I face [company name]. I will meet the challenge and welcome it for I am a gladiator.

    This was just another idea to be different. I couldn't believe it. I would look up "creative cover letter" on the internet and get... cover letters. Nothing creative about them.

The Ten Reasons Cover Letter

Ten reasons [company name] should assimilate me.

Ten: I smile a lot. It's good for morale.
Nine: I walked away, literally, from a snowboarding accident that tore my spleen in half. Compared to that, a stressful month at work is nothing.
Eight: Kids like me.
Seven: I have a genetic predisposition to optimism.
Six: When I don't know how to do something that needs to be done, I learn how.
Five: I strategically start sentences with the word "Dude" creating an instant icebreaker and giving me time to compose my thoughts while the other party giggles.
Four: If I'm ever angry you can diffuse it by making me laugh due to my being accursedly ticklish.
Three: I am low maintenance. Eight square hours of sleep a night and surfing once a week and it's all good.
Two: I enjoy cooking. I have been known to bring dinner for my coworkers.
One: I'm a very creative writer.

And, if these random facts don't have you just salivating to have me on the team I would be more than happy to submit some writing samples.

Many of the short stories that I wrote were intended to be used for my father's storytelling ministry. If memory serves me right, which often it doesn't, most of them were written around 2004 and 2005 while I was in Long Beach trying to figure my life out after earning my BA.

The change to writing short stories was about the fourth change I had made in my writing focus over a period of about six years. At first the goal had been a novel, then original feature film, and for a short time adaptation of a novel or videogame to film.

This first story, Bus Stop, was a cannibalization of a movie script idea I had started writing back in high school. By the end of all the rewrites about the only thing that stayed the same was that the story begins on a bus.

Bus Stop

Not too far from here there is a small town. It is an average, everyday sort of town, probably much like the one you grew up in. The thing that sets this town apart from any other town is that there is only one road out and it is a road traveled by a single bus. Everyday, as the sun begins to set, the bus stops at the station. Since it is the only bus people of all sorts are forced to share the ride. They are young and old, rich and poor.

It is on this bus that a rich, young man sits next to an old woman in rags.

"Where are you headed?" the old woman asks.

"The end of the line," is the man's reply.

"Oh, why?" the woman asks concerned.

"Because I'm taking the bus to the city," the rich man says, looking for another place to sit, but all the seats are full giving him no place to move to.

"But the bus doesn't go to the city," the woman says. "It stops outside the city. You have to get off and walk. You should come with me."

"Why would I want to walk with you?" the man says looking at her clothes disdainfully.

17

The woman looks at the rich man with sad eyes. She is silent for a moment. Then, forcing a smile, replies.

"If you don't get off at the next stop you will miss the city. It's the only way to get there."

"I already said I was going to ride the bus to the city, not some ratty out-of-town stop. Now, leave me alone. Let me ride along in peace." The man turns his back on the woman.

"But sir,"

The rich man stands, cutting her off and moves down the aisle offering people money in exchange for their seat. Finally a young boy takes the money and sits next to the old woman.

The boy gives the old woman a wary look. She smiles at him and scoots over to give him as much room on the seat as she can. After a few minutes of silence, the woman, unable to stay quiet, speaks.

"Where are you going?"

"Not sure," the boy replies, "doesn't matter."

"Oh, why doesn't it matter?" the woman asks.

"Because I'm out of town. I just wanted to ride the bus."

"But you are so young. You can't just leave town with nowhere to go," the woman replies. "Why don't you get off at my stop and you can stay with me?"

"I don't want to stay with you. I don't even know you," the boy says giving the woman a look that says she is crazy, "I'm not getting off the bus. The further I ride it and the longer I'm away from home the better."

"You can't just ride the bus," the woman says.

"Why not?" the boy asks a bit concerned.

The woman is about to reply when another passenger interrupts.

"Lady why don't you leave him alone. You're starting to scare the kid?"

"He should be scared," the woman says without looking away from the boy. "You all should."

"Forget this," the boy says as he gets up. He heads up the aisle and wedges himself between two teenage girls, almost pushing one off her seat. The girl is forced to take his seat next to the old woman.

"Just… don't talk to me," the girl tells the old woman.

The old woman tries not to speak, but again it becomes too hard to stay silent.

"Where are you taking the bus?" the old woman asks.

"I'm taking the bus to the mountains where my friends took it. We're going to have a huge party there." the girl insists. With that she gets up and stands in the aisle.

The woman waits, but no one comes to sit next to her. Hurt, the woman stands and begins asking others if they would get off the bus at the stop before the city with her. They all refuse. Some say that all the stops are the same, others that her stop makes it harder to get where they are going. Some tell her to just enjoy the ride.

Finally, the bus comes to a stop next to a single pole at the head of a dirt road. Everyone watches the old woman climb slowly out of the bus and walk down the road alone. The bus pulls away from the stop and drives on and an amazing thing happens as the passengers watch.

The woman's stooped shoulders straighten, the color returns to her hair, and her old, wrinkled skin becomes firm and bright. Her tattered rags flutter in the wind. They are no longer rags, but a magnificent gown. Others appear on the road to greet the woman with hugs and cries. Between one step and the next the dirt road becomes a boardwalk flanked by beautiful scenery at the end of which is a golden gate.

Then the woman is lost from sight as the bus curves toward the city.

"See," says the rich man, "we're getting to the city faster than her."

But then they are passing the city. The road curves away toward the mountains and the city is left far behind. The mountains rise ahead of them and there are no more stops, no places to escape.

When the bus reaches the mountains it enters a long dark tunnel, so long and so dark that the bus never comes out again. There is no party there. The passengers wail and tear at doors that will not open. They hammer at windows that will not break. They beg a driver that will not stop.

    Imprisoned the passengers starve and suffer.
Their clothes become rags. Their youth fades.
Always on and on into the darkness they go. The
next night another bus stops in the town and picks
up many passengers, but none get to the city. Few
ever get to the city.

This one was for my father. I was looking at his life and wanted to do something that had meaning as well as paid tribute to what he had been through over the years.

Mountain Top

He stood on a mountain top. A man, young, healthy and strong. His skin sun-bronzed and eyes shining bright. He wore simple clothes and his short, dark hair glistened in the sun and floated on the breeze.

"What shall I do?" the man asked. From the sky came a firm yet gentle voice.

"Go."

The man looked down into the valley where it was shadowed and dark.

"Go," the voice urged.

Powerful legs carried the young man quickly from the peak. He passed into the trees without pause. Rays of light filtered through the branches onto the man's path. Deeper into the forest he passed. Slowly the trees grew thicker blocking out more and more of the sun. The way became darker and colder.

The man stopped for a moment in the last, faint ray of light. He saw the path before him disappearing into deep darkness. He was a long, long way from the mountain top.

"What shall I do?" the man asked.

"Go," the voice commanded. So the man traveled on.

Behind him the ray of light faded as the sun set. Brambles began to encroach on the path before him. It became more and more difficult to keep his way.

Then the path was gone. The trees grew in tight. The undergrowth became a wicked tangle, one branch twining into the next. The man was forced to fight his way dodging limbs when he could, but bending and breaking them as often as not. They in turn tore at his clothes and his skin. When the man found himself in a tangle that he could not pass or break through he had to turn back, being scratched and torn as much getting out as he had in. A cold wind began blowing through the trees. The man began to tire of his journey.

"What shall I do?" he asked, but there was no answer. So, he rushed on. Suddenly, the man was out of the trees. He stood on the bank of a river. The moonlight shone on the water, and the man knelt to drink. When he did he saw his reflection.

It was a stranger's reflection that the man saw. Leaves and twigs twined in tattered clothes, hair grown long was whipped by the wind instead of floating on the breeze. A wild gray beard covered a scarred and scratched, pale and worn face. Yet, there was a remembrance of the light from the mountain top in his eyes.

"I will go on," the man said. He stood and waded into the river. Cold enveloped his legs and seeped into his body. He began to shiver as the water swept up around his waist and the current began pulling. When the water ran over his chest the man struck out swimming. Stroke after stroke he fought the current striving for the other side.

His arms began to ache. His shoulders burned. His soaked clothes drew him down. He struggled to even catch a breath while shivering and crying tears of pain. On and on, until he could swim no more. As he sank, even as despair set in, the man held his breath, fighting.

Then his foot struck the muddy bottom. His lungs burning, the man took a step forward and then another. Too tired to swim he walked on the bottom of the river.

Then, with another step, his head broke the surface and he drew in a ragged breath. He struggled out of the river falling to his knees and crawling forward through the mud, coughing water and clutching his shivering, aching body.

"Go," the whispered remembrance of the voice called the man to his feet. On into the forest once again the man surged. Cold wind bit through his muddy, tattered and soaked rags. He continued to cough, wracked by sickness and pain. On through the brush and brambles he raced. Exhaustion overcame him. The stones underfoot began to break away causing him to stumble and slow. He fell to his knees and crawled his way over sharp rocks that tore at his hands and knees. Weary and old, tired and bleeding, cold and sick, ever onward he went, though even now the memory of the light was gone.

And then it was over. The man found himself atop another mountain. Through all his agony and grief he had not realized that he had been climbing. Now he stood on a high peak above even the clouds, cold, tired, and bleeding.

"Why," the man asked, "why did I have to go?"

As he stood there the wind died and the sun rose. Light so bright the man had to shield his face warmed his cold, tired, bleeding body.

"Because, your mountain was not high enough. Mine is," The voice said out of the light.

"What shall I do?" the man asked no longer sick and tired. No longer old and aching, no longer cold and weary.

"Stay. Your journey is done and you are home."

This story aggravated me to no end. It is often the simplest thing that will make the greatest impact in a story. This story was missing one of those simple things. It took my dad .6 seconds to come up with the perfect line that it was missing.

A Surfer's Christmas

It was a cold winter morning. Three surfers crossed a lonely stretch of beach. The only sound was the ever-present tumble of whitewater as it foamed its way toward the shore and then receded back to the sea.

Dawn's first glow was beginning to brighten the sky as the surfers waded into the water and began catching wave after wave. The sun rose for a mere moment, a brief instant of perfection and then it was gone. A thin fog from off in the distance rolled across the sun, casting the world into murkiness.

The world changed. The water and the sky merged into a flat, gray plane where nothing was quite what it should be. Despite the change the surfers continued catching waves, paying no mind as the thickening fog rolled over them onto shore.

Soon, the beach became a hazy, half-seen stretch of sand. The sounds of the breaking waves and the surfer's splashes were dulled by the haze, but they kept surfing as the shore was lost to gray.

Then came the lull. They sat and waited for the next set, telling stories of past days and listening to the dull crash of the waves behind them pushing toward an unseen shore. All this time they hadn't seen that a current was silently pulling them out to sea.

All was quiet. They realized that they could no longer hear any waves. Like the fog, fear crept over them. Without sight and sound they had no way to tell which was the way back to shore. Any way they went could take them further from land.

They sat on their boards, huddled together and very alone. Lost. Every so often one would think he heard a wave crash or that he had caught a glimpse of land and would paddle in that direction, but never more than a few yards. The sound would never be repeated, the sight would never reappear, and his hope would die so he would turn back and rejoin his companions.

Lost and adrift they could be miles out to sea before the fog cleared. They began to despair. Then, ready to give up hope, they heard a sound.

It was a sound like no other on earth. It had the power to carry any distance, cut through any barrier, and call to any one. It was the piercing cry of a child.

As one, they struck out toward the cries. They paddled as fast as they could. Their arms tired; their hearts raced. On and on they paddled, urging and encouraging one another. When it seemed that they could paddle no more the water swelled beneath them and waves began pushing them to the beach. They rode all the way to shore and left their boards on the sand to seek the source of the cries. There, on the beach, they found a young mother, a woman off the streets who had just given birth to a son.

They ran to their cars and brought back gifts. Using their hot water bottles they bathed the child. They wrapped mother and child in their clean, dry clothes and fed the hungry mother from their lunches. Warm and clean the child stopped crying and his mother cradled her son in her arms. The surfers gazed in wonder at the face of their savior. My friends, this was not the first time a child had come to save the lost.

Not all of my writing was for my father's ministry. When I was really focused on trying to get into advertising I started writing commercials.

A quick brush up for those who haven't read a movie script. They are written in the present tense and only what the audience can see is described.

1: When reading a script the setting is announced by a single line that is in all caps. It gives a prepositional location (interior or exterior) followed by a specific location (party, John's house, beach) and then the time is separated by a hyphen.

2: New characters that we haven't seen are indicated by all caps. 2a: This character appeared previously.

3: Sound effects come in all caps.

4: A character's name is given and then their dialogue follows directly under.

(1)EXT CEMETERY GRAVE SITE - LATER

The cemetery is empty except for (2)SARAH walking towards the grave. She stops when she is in almost the same spot as (2a)Annie had been.

Sarah pulls a tissue wrapped object out of her pocket and unwraps it carefully. She kneels and whispers GOODBYE as she places a glass rose on the grave.

INT ANNIE'S HOUSE - EVENING

People mill about the house. Some carry small plates of food, others sit talking quietly. Annie converses with an older woman, TARA, in the hall next to the kitchen.

                    (4)TARA
        Sam couldn't get leave. I'm so
        sorry he wasn't here.

                        ANNIE
            It probably hurts Sam worse that
            he couldn't be here.

There is a (3)DING from the kitchen.

It's hard for me to write something that doesn't have a message. Ever since I wrote this public service announcement I have had the Scarecrow's song from "The Wizard of Oz" stuck in my head. Seriously. I whistle it all the time.

Public Service Announcement

INT PARTY - EVENING

Everything is in black and white at this point. The guests are dancing, drinking, and generally having a good time. A man, TIM, gets a drink.

Tim walks over to a woman. Flashing her a silly grin he puts his arm around her shoulders and says something to her. We don't hear what is said, but it's pretty blatant that he gets shot down when she brushes his hand off and walks away. However, the silly grin remains on his face.

Tim gets up on a table, does a little dance with drink in hand, drains his drink, and bows to the small crowd. He stumbles drunkenly from the room.

EXT HOUSE - EVENING

Tim takes a while to get in his car and drives off swerving drunkenly.

EXT OVERPASS - EVENING

The car swerves down the road far too fast and crashes into one of the supports for the overpass. A bystander screams.

EXT OVERPASS - MOMENTS LATER

A SIREN APPROACHES. An ambulance appears and EMT's make their way through the crowd.

The EMT's pull Tim out of the wreck.

They stick Tim on a stretcher and hoist him into the ambulance.

INT HOSPITAL - EVENING

The DOCTOR takes one look at TIM and pulls his
surgical mask down, shaking his head.

                              FADE OUT:

                              FADE IN:

EXT GRAVEYARD - DAY

Now everything is in color. There are many ornate
gravestones, and what appears to be a SCARECROW
planted at a fresh grave.

As we get closer we see that it is really Tim
dressed and mounted as a scarecrow. He begins to
sing to the tune of "If I Only Had A Brain."

                    TIM
          All the thoughts I'd be thinkin',
          if I had not been drinkin', if I
          only had a brain.
                              FADE TO BLACK.

I like commercials because they are fast. Thirty seconds to a minute is all you get to tell a whole story. It has to have something that really sticks with the audience, something unexpected.

Car Commercial

EXT BANK - DAY

Parked in front of the bank in a very high-class neighborhood is the TARGET VEHICHLE.

The voice over lists all the vehicles attributes, starting with the luxuries and getting slowly more technical, eventually touching on the handling and, finally, horse-power.

While the voice over narrates life in the neighborhood passes by as usual.

- A woman walks her poodle past the vehicle.

- Two children run around the vehicle shooting each other with water guns.

- A man walks by talking on his cell phone.

As the voice over gets closer to the technical aspects of the vehicle a SIREN starts up in the distance and grows louder.

               V.O.
     And an amazing 350 horse-power
     motor.

Several masked men run out of the bank waving guns and carrying bags of cash. They jump in the vehicle and speed off.

Several police cars speed by in pursuit and the neighborhood is returned to calm.

                    V.O.
          Not quite what we thought you'd
          use it for.

One of the best examples of a good commercial theme is the MasterCard commercials. They are fun, probably relatively inexpensive to shoot, and even if you forget the specifics, the product stays in your mind.

MasterCard Commercial: That Look

INT HOUSE - DAY

The calendar on the wall says January. TYLER becomes visible in the shot for a second and then drops out. His push-ups take him in and out of the shot.

> VOICE OVER
> Ten thousand push ups... zero dollars.

INT HOUSE - DAY

The Calendar says March. Tyler is now doing sit-ups.

> VOICE OVER
> Twenty thousand sit ups... zero dollars.

EXT HILL - DAY

Tyler comes running over the hill.

> VOICE OVER
> One thousand miles... zero dollars.

Tyler reaches his house. He strips off his sweaty shirt and walks in.

INT TYLER'S HOUSE - DAY

                         TYLER'S MOM
                           (O.C.)
                Tyler, come meet our new
                neighbors.

INT - FAMILY ROOM

Tyler's MOM is sitting with two incredibly
gorgeous girls Tyler's age. They both openly check
Tyler out, liking what they see.

                         VOICE OVER
                Getting that look... priceless.
                There are some things money can't
                buy. For everything else there's
                MasterCard.

For this commercial I used Dial since it was the soap that was in the bathroom at the time. I figured it would work for any soap, especially Axe.

Soap Commercial

INT RESTAURANT - EVENING

ANDY and TRISH sit in an Italian restaurant having a wonderful date in the early evening. Trish giggles at what Andy just said.

                    TRISH
  No way.

                    ANDY
  Come on go for it.

Andy opens his mouth. Trish scoops a meatball off her plate of spaghetti with her spoon. She uses her spoon as a catapult to fling the meatball at Andy's mouth. It bounces off his neck and both laugh. He wipes the sauce off, but misses a little bit.

EXT ANDY'S HOUSE - LATER

Andy and Trish kiss in the darkness. They separate and then Andy hops up the steps into the light. He has lipstick smudges on his face and the spaghetti sauce stain is still on his neck.

                    ANDY
  I'll see you later.

                    TRISH
  Ok.

Andy enters his house.

INT ANDY'S HOUSE BATHROOM - MOMENTS LATER

Andy checks out the lipstick smudges and the spaghetti sauce stain in the mirror. He strips down and hops in the shower, where he lathers up with DIAL soap.

INT ANDY'S HOUSE BEDROOM - MOMENTS LATER

Andy finishes dressing and leaves his house.

EXT NEW HOUSE - LATER

Andy knocks on the door. It opens and a different girl, LISA stands there obviously surprised.

                    LISA
    Hi babe, how was guys night? Do
    anything special?

                    ANDY
    No.

                    ANNOUNCER (V.O.)
    Dial, with an invigorating scent
    and superior cleaning power it
    cleans everything, but your
    conscience.

Commercials weren't the only short scripts I tried out. The Devil and the Salesman came out of a project pops and I started before he got sick: Pastor's Helper.

This was the first time I had done a script for on-stage. The format is wrong but it's readable so ttthhhhbbp.

The Devil and the Salesman

The Devil is onstage. A salesman enters from the side and mimes knocking on the door. KNOCKING. The Devil answers the door.

SSM: Good afternoon sir.

DEVIL: Who in Hades are you?

SSM: I am just a humble salesman.

DEVIL: Well, go away. I don't want anything from you.

SSM: Are you sure?

DEVIL: Yes.

SSM: Too bad. I have here the finest innovation in deception since the lie.

DEVIL: Really, cause that was my greatest work.

SSM: To be sure, but that was several millennia ago. Let me ask you a question. Are you tired of constantly having to deceive believers?

DEVIL: Am I ever.

SSM: Well then, what if I told you I have a program here that will put a stop to all your struggles?

DEVIL: Are you trying to sell me some dressed up deceit?

SSM: At it's core, yes, but it's something very different. What do you say? Six payments of sixty-six dollars. No shipping.

DEVIL: Why don't you tell me more and we'll see.

SSM: I usually don't give out free material, but you're a nice guy. I like you. What I'm gonna do for you is tell you about why this program works. It's simple really. The most believable lie has the most truth to it.

DEVIL: Tell me something I don't know.

SSM: So, what we have done is taken that tried and true principle and mixed it with the unexpected. You with me?

DEVIL: I'm listening.

SSM: So, we teach your targets about. . . Jesus.

DEVIL: What!?

SSM: I know. You're going to say. That that's crazy.

DEVIL: Because that's crazy!

SSM: Stay with me for a bit. What makes your job so hard?

DEVIL: God.

SSM: And why is that?

DEVIL: Because when people submit to Him they change.

SSM: So how do you keep them from changing?

DEVIL: Keep them from learning about Jesus.

SSM: Wrong. Just think of the effort that would take. Besides, the Word always gets out.

DEVIL: There's always danger, threats, and force. I could send my minions to-

SSM: Still too much effort. Why not get them to <u>not change</u> of their own free will?

DEVIL: How would I do that without force?

SSM: By teaching Jesus.

DEVIL: That makes no sense at all.

SSM: Well, when people give their lives to God they change. If they think they have done what they need to without giving their lives up to God, if they don't die to themselves, then they won't change. Teach them to ask Jesus into their heart so that he will change them.

DEVIL: But if he comes into their lives-

SSM: That's just it. He won't come into their lives because they don't open the door. The redeeming work of Jesus does no good until a person begins to obey him

DEVIL: So I get them to ask him in and then they'll think that they have done what they need to do and are ok?

SSM: Exactly. Instead of taking up their cross daily they just ask him in once

	and think that is it. So, shall we talk pricing?
DEVIL:	What should I pay you for? You just laid out your program.
SSM:	Ah, but I haven't given you all the trappings.
DEVIL:	What are those?
SSM:	They are all the other distractions. Things where people think that by saying the right words and observing the right rituals, and going to the right classes, that they have their life squared away. The Sinner's Prayer, the sacraments of Baptism and Communion, Catechism, Confirmation, Church Membership. Sprinkle them around in the denominations. Without dying to themselves it all amounts to them standing behind a locked door shouting for the knocker to come in.
DEVIL:	Yes, let's talk pricing.

While taking film classes at Long Beach we were given some really interesting assignments. One was to have a character being interrogated by another based solely on the fact that everyone is guilty of something. It didn't have to be a formal interrogation. I think the first time I did the assignment I had a leaf interrogating the tree that it was going to fall from.

I love the cheesy "serious business" line.

Interrogation

The two men sat across from each other at a stone table in the park. One of them, the one with the wispy gray hair and glasses, adjusted a folder in front of him. He had on a fresh suit; his jacket was unbuttoned to allow his ample stomach freedom as he sat. The other simply wore faded blue jeans and a white tee-shirt. The jeans were not the color you get at the store, but the color you can only get by wearing them day after day, out in the sun, running in them, working in them, wiping your hands on them, staining them, and cleaning them.

"My name," the one in the suit said, "is Carl. And I know who you are, Adam. I know who you have been, what you've done. I know everything there is to know about you." He placed his hand on the file in front of him. Adam kept his gaze on Carl's eyes and shrugged.

"Good for you."

"I have statements about you, witnesses. I've done my research. I know you better than your own mother knows you," Carl sneered.

"You could," Adam admitted. "It's not likely, but you might. More than likely you don't know me at all."

Two children came running around a stone wall. Adam turned his gaze to watch them. They were playing make believe. One held his arms out above his head in tiny fists while he ran and made whooshing sounds.

"I'll get you Lex Luthor."

Carl kept his gaze locked where it had been. He didn't allow his eyes to wander. Intently he studied Adam. When Adam turned back Carl's eyes tried to burrow into him. Adam was unfazed by the scrutiny. Giving up on that Carl looked down at the file. He flipped it open and began skimming through the pages. He sort of mumbled as he read.

"Do you really think there is anything in there that can help you?" Adam quietly asked the question. It wasn't a resigned quiet. It wasn't a worried quiet. It wasn't a reverent quiet, merely a calm quiet.

"There is everything in here. For instance you were born May 16, 1976." The glimmer of a bead of sweat was starting to show on Carl's forehead.

"So you know that I am thirty."

Carl wiped the sweat from his forehead. He gave Adam a smug look.

"You are thirty. I am fifty-seven. I have almost twice the life experience you do. That means in this battle of wits you are going to lose."

"I didn't know this was a battle of wits."

Carl blew his breath out his nose.

"I didn't know I had anything to lose. I thought we were here for a reason."

"We are here for a reason, and I know what you are trying to do."

Adam remained silent. He glanced at the children still playing their game. Now Superman was on his knees weakly trying to fend off Lex Luthor.

"You come to our world invincible, but I have the key to killing you."

Carl followed Adam's gaze. His mind cranked trying to puzzle out what Adam was thinking. What could two children with their childish game have to do with what they were here for? Adam stopped watching the kids and watched Carl watch them. Carl watched for quite a while.

"I wonder who is going to win." Adam's words shook Carl out of his trancelike analysis.

Carl glared at Adam. He had been caught off guard and he hated that. He snapped a reply in anger at Adam and then wished he hadn't.

"No one wins! No one ever wins! Superman will capture Lex Luthor and put him in jail, but then he escapes! He always escapes! No one would want to play him if he didn't!" Carl cleared his throat. "Getting back to the business at hand I'd like to get started."

"We hadn't already started?"

"Look," Carl said, trying to keep his temper under control, "this is not a game to me. It may be to you, but not to me."

Adam nodded to the kids playing their game. "They play a game, we do not."

Carl's eyes narrowed at Adam.

Adam shrugged.

"We have business to attend to."

"Business?" Carl asked.

"Would you prefer I call it something else? You may want to call it by another name, but that doesn't change the fact of what it is. An interrogation is an interrogation, whether you call it business, a game, or a test."

Carl tapped the folder.

"Then let us call it business, serious business."

Carl's statement hovered there between them. He watched to see what kind of effect it had on Adam. He was dissatisfied that it didn't seem to affect him one way or another. Adam continued to watch Carl.

"I don't wanna be Lex Luthor any more. I wanna be Superman. I wanna fly."

The children's voices drifted into the silence. Carl shifted his weight on the bench.

"You know," Carl said, "I can wait as long as you. Why don't you go ahead and talk."

"What should we talk about?" Adam asked.

"May 13, 1996."

"What about it?" Adam shrugged.

"You tell me."

Adam sniffed. He tapped his nose with his index finger in thought.

"Not really much to tell. The whole deal took about three minutes. I didn't really do much. Everyone else had him so messed up that it was basically over by the time I took my shot. If you only count what I did it took about six seconds."

The click of high heels on the cement pulled Adam's attention. He looked over his shoulder. Walking down the path in the park was a pair of dark shapely legs that went way up and up into a tight skirt. Adam let his head roll to his other shoulder following her progress. She was approached by a man who embraced her. He was the kind of man that had a fat wallet, a fast car, and stock good looks.

"Lucky man," Adam said.

"Lucky man," Carl agreed. He flipped through the folder. "Tell me about-

"I wonder if he thinks he's lucky." Carl glared at Adam's interruption. "I mean it's not every guy who gets a woman like that. It's only a guy like that who gets a woman like that."

"I wouldn't know. I'm not a guy like that." Carl said.

"No, you're not."

A small breeze brought a floating puff ball between the two men. It drifted between them for a moment. On a sudden whim of the breeze it changed direction and touched Carl.

"Quick, make a wish Carl."

"What?"

"Make a wish. You were touched now you make a wish. What do you want? It can be anything. Maybe to beat me at the game? To be smart enough to beat me. Something else maybe? You want to be something else, someone else? Maybe you want to be that guy with the girl?"

Carl slammed the file shut.

"I do not want to be that man!"

"Why not?"

"Because," Carl ground his teeth, "he is stupid. If it wasn't for his thick wallet, his three hours a day in the gym, and the absolute fallacy that he represents, he wouldn't have a chance with her! He has the I.Q. of a slug. I'd take brains over what he has any day."

"So then you want to be smart. That's why you compiled a file on me. That's what smart people do. They have all the information. They know everything. They can't be wrong."

"They are never wrong," Carl spat. "Yes I want to be someone smarter."

"You want to be someone smarter, not you want to be smarter. Someone else. You wish you were someone who isn't you."

44

Carl knew then. He had said it. It was true. Carl hated being who he was. He wished more than anything that he was someone else.

"What about them?" Carl asked pointing at the kids.

"They are playing a game." Adam answered getting up. He dusted off the bottom of his jeans. "They want to be Superman today and Batman tomorrow, and whatever takes their fancy the next day, but deep down they want to be themselves. Sadly their day will come. They will face it as well and I will leave them with this same admonition. Know thy self."

Broadening my horizons further I have even gone into designing several video games. I'm not a big fan of the format for presenting them, but I can appreciate how practical it is for what it does.

Hades Sent

Title: Hades Sent - Working Title

Genre: Third-Person ¾ View Action-Adventure

Version: 1

The Idea: Alcander makes a deal with Hades, to ensure that his wife Damara ends up in paradise and Hades doesn't hold up his end of the bargain. Alcander unleashes hell in Hades' realm. He must travel from the Pit of Tartaus past Charon, the River Styx, and Cerberus to rescue his wife from the Asphodel Fields.
Getting to his wife is only half the battle. They still have to pass through Hades' home and personal guards, and that is only after Alcander manages to remind Damara who he is.

Category: Hades Sent should have a general control like that of Diablo or The Legend of Zelda, with the ability to enter first person point-of-view for precision shots. Gear will be opportunistic. Alcander will pick up several items that may help him in his quest. These items will give advantages such as range or power, but it will be up to the player and their use of the items that will maximize the benefits.

Platforms: Nintendo Wii. The motion sensitive controller would allow players to move a weapon to one side or the other, as in a block, and then strike out of that position, creating more than a generic slash attack for each weapon. An attack to the feet will have a different effect than an attack to the arm holding a weapon or the head.

License: Hades Sent is an original intellectual property with great potential to become a licensed franchise. Greek mythology is fraught with the interactions of the gods and mortals. Though mortals age and die, the gods are ever present. In their own way the gods were as flawed as mortals, but far more powerful. The franchise would be a series of games that would explore these flaws. Hades was deceitful. Another game could focus on Zeus's arrogance, Hera's jealousy, Poseidon's wrath, Nemesis's vengeance, Prometheus's compassion for humanity. The franchise would be a modern day pantheon.

Play Mechanics: The player will control Alcander from the darkest depths of Hades. He will fight his way through the underworld using whatever he can get his hands on as a weapon. For the times that out-right combat would be ineffectual Alcander will crawl, run, jump, swim, hide, and sneak his way past opponents.

Target Audience: Hades Sent targets the 12-25 gamer, both male and female. The story is a love story, but it has enough action to satisfy any guy or girl's battle hunger. The setting of the underworld is also such that it captures the imagination of both men and women.

Unique Selling Points: As part of elementary education all students study Greek mythology at about sixth grade. However, their study is generally watered down and superficial. It leaves kids wondering. Hades Sent - and further licensed games - would capitalize on that curiosity. Although learning would not be the focus of the game they can not help learn when they encounter Sisyphus or Prometheus in the under world.
There is also a darkness about the game based on its setting in the underworld. However, the scene and tortures are neither overly gory, nor disgustingly dark. Ixion spinning on the fiery wheel, Sisyphus, ever pushing his rock uphill, Pierithous forever attached to his chair, and Tantalus by the pool he can not drink from and the tree he can not eat from are all side characters that will grab the gamers attention.

Marketing Summary: Our media has become so focused on the dangers of terrorism and gas prices, it's all kids are hearing about. Hades Sent will do well because it offers something old and generally forgotten after the grade school test, seen with a new light.

Game Overview: Hades Sent

Hades is visiting his brother Poseidon. Hades continues to hint that people are not giving his brother his due. It has been too long since any but those that sailed the seas paid homage to the mighty Poseidon. Poseidon is convinced to send a storm to ravage the land and remind people of his deity. The storm tears from the sea across the land. Many souls are sent to Hades that night.

Alcander's wife, Damara, sends him out to check on the widow Alatea. When he gets to her house he finds her snoring away, oblivious to the storm. In a good humor, he returns home as the height of the storm hits. Alcander arrives just in time to watch his house come crashing down upon his wife. He tears across the yard and searches desperately through the rubble. He finds his wife alive, but fading fast.

Alcander can not bear it when Damara begins to say her goodbyes. He calls out into the storm for Hades, who appears out of the night. Alcander begs Hades to spare the life of his loved one. Hades regrets that he can't just let a soul go. Alcander takes the hint and offers his soul to Tartarus then, for the assurance that his wife will live and enter the Elysian Fields when the time comes. Hades accepts the offer and takes Alcander down across the river Styx, past Cerberus, and into the land of the dead.

As part of Alcander's torture he is not forced to drink from the pool of Lethe and forget all his memories of life. Hades wants him to remember his wife and know that he will never be with her. Hades leaves Alcander free to roam Tartarus. Alcander, while accompanying Sisyphus up his hill spies Damara, not in the Elysian Fields, but in the Fields of Asphodel and boils with anger. He vows that his agreement with Hades has been betrayed so he has no obligation to remain in Tartarus. He sets out to escape the pit. Sisyphus suggests that since the river Phelegthon flows into Tartarus, it can be followed out.

Alcander heads for the river of fire. Not one to give up denizens easily the Pit of Tartarus raises up foul creatures to bar Alcander's way. Climbing through caverns on the banks of the Phelegthon Alcander slogs through demons. At long last he climbs over the rim of the pit. Sisyphus salutes him from the top of his hill, and for once, starts after his stone with a hint of a smile.

Alcander is not done with the fiery river. Having no way to cross it he must follow the river until it leads him to the shores of the unburied dead. They will do all they can to destroy him before Charon appears to ferry souls across the river Styx. Once Charon arrives the unburied dead fall back. Charon demands the toll from Alcander. Alcander has no toll to pay him, but vows that he will be on the ferry.

At this, an epic battle ensues. When Charon has been defeated he compliments Alcander. The fight was merely Charon's way of testing him. Charon apologizes that he is unable to take Alcander across, but he hints that Alcander can cross the marsh that the River Styx runs over. He tells Alcander of a relatively safe path that runs along where the river Styx and Phelegthon converge.

While crossing this treacherous fjord, Alcander is confronted by the souls of those caught in the river. They are allowed exit for a short time to drag any attempting to cross to their watery prison.

After managing to avoid being dragged to a hideous fate, Alcander must cross The Plains of Judgment where he is tested by Minos. Both battles and puzzles will be used to test his mettle. When Alcander has proven himself, Minos takes him to the Vale of Mourning. Before Minos leaves Alcander he reveals that Alcander is not dead.

The denizens of the Vale of Mourning are loathe to allow any of the living past their realm. At its end of the vale Alcander faces Cerberus, the three-headed canine guard of the underworld. Defeating Cerberus gains him entrance into the Asphodel Fields where he is faced with the task of finding his wife among the other souls. He must chase her wandering path through the Asphodel fields.

The reunion with his wife is bittersweet since Damara has drunk from the river Lethe and has no memory. Eris, the mother of Lethe, appears. She strikes a bargain with Alcander. If he will bring her a branch from the Elm From Which Hang False Dreams, she will force her daughter Lethe to restore Damara's memories.

To retrieve this branch Alcander must venture to the far south of Hades' realm. Here the rushing waters, burning fires, and screams from Tartarus are all left behind. Alcander must pass the Shades of Abandon that bar the way to the tree. To be allowed to take a limb from the tree Alcander must solve several insidious puzzles.

Once he has the limb from the tree and is heading back Eris appears. She takes the limb and disappears. When Alcander returns to the Fields of Asphodel Eris is nowhere to be found. Alcander heads for the pool of Lethe to drink himself. When he gets there Lethe questions why a living mortal would seek to drink from the water of her pool. Alcander tells his tale and Lethe tells him that her mother spreads mischief. Lethe restores Damara's memory and wishes them luck.

Alcander and Damara will then face the daunting task of the road that leads to Hades' Palace. They must make their way through Hades' immense home, past the Hundred-Handed, to the gates of the Elysian Fields. There they are faced with the greatest horror of all. Hades himself bars their way. If Alcander can not defeat him he will not die, he will cease to have ever existed.

Fantasy games aren't the only genre I attempted.

Codename - Traveler

Title: Codename - Traveler

Genre: FPS

Version 1

The Big Idea: When you are an operative doing things for a government that would be politically damaging if the truth ever came out, you run the risk of being hung out to dry. Couple that with the fact that there are people that will do anything for money and power and it makes the danger of running a hush-hush operation alone and overseas only for the top elite few. You are Traveler, a black-ops agent, one of the few on just such a mission. A ten year long mission that is almost complete.
Things degenerate when you are sold out by someone on your own side and the government denies all ties to you. Most would just bug out, but being who and what you are, you aren't leaving until this mission is accomplished.

Category: A fast paced action adventure along the lines of Counter Strike, but incorporating the intrigue and twists offered in a James Bond film.

Platforms: Xbox 360, PS3, PC.

License/ Franchise: Codename: Traveler is an original intellectual property. A ten year, under-cover mission, would create interesting prequel possibilities due to a whole decade of change, and the possibilities for a sequel are there as well. What will the senator do before he is taken down by the government? Will terrorists try and reach Traveler in the United States? Will Traveler want to stay where the system is so corrupt, or go back to where his fight can truly help people? What did

Traveler do to be chosen for such an extended mission? The answers to these questions would be found in a protracted series of games.

    Play Mechanic: Most of the game takes place with the player on foot. There is a section where the player must drive a vehicle. Other than that it is a fairly standard, walk, run, jump, crouch, fire weapon, use item, switch weapon first-person shooter control setup. Efficiency in fire fights will be a stressed mechanic. Spray and pray is a very last resort. Tactical decisions would also be paramount. Out think the enemy. If the player was firing from a doorway and then creeps to a window the enemy would still be focused on the door giving the player enough time to aim and take a good shot.

    Target Audience: Males age 15-35 that are into first-person shooters should be chomping at the bit to get their hands on this game. They will be familiar with the controls, and ideas, but surprised at the realism in tactics.

    Unique Selling Points: The story emphasizes that the best laid plans often go horribly wrong. Throughout the game the player is trying to go undetected and un-noticed, but it just never seems to work. The action becomes incidental as opposed to forced, which helps the player suspend their disbelief and really get into the game.
Codename - Traveler also capitalizes on the Lone Wolf mentality. Traveler has nothing to support him overseas and when he is sold out, home soil isn't safe either.

    Game Overview: Codename: Traveler

    The game starts with a junker speeding through the Afgahni desert. The camera circles the vehicle getting closer until transferring to a 1st person POV. You must drive your vehicle to a set navigation point. After doing so you must climb the rocks at your destination. From the top of the rocks you set up a directional microphone and binoculars to gather information. What you witness is the meeting of several heads of terrorist cells.

The gist of the meeting is that while staying as small fractured cells these "freedom fighters" are safe, yet weak. Their efforts are neither gaining ground nor losing it. Their countrymen have felt the presence of the infidel on their home soil for long enough. It is time that the western devils felt the pain of a fight in their homeland. The one man who could unite them and carry out this plan, the one that the United States would give its First Amendment, so to speak, to catch, needs to meet with the heads of as many cells as he can. The meeting will take place in two days, and no one other than a leader is to know about it. All leaders are to leave their body guards out of the loop. Their contact has been sent with the personal assurance of Hadiem that they will be protected.

Having learned where and when the greatest threat to the United States is going to be gathered together, you must get back to home in time for work or risk blowing your cover.

The next day at your job you notice there are several people hanging around the area that don't seem to have any reason to be there. Your boss sends you out on an errand and the men follow you. It becomes pretty evident that these people are looking for the right time and place to either capture or kill you. And, they are presented with it. You come to a deserted alley that you must go down to complete the errand.

After fighting off these thugs you must hide. A young woman at the mouth of the alley misdirects other pursuers. She tells them that you fled through her house and others. After they leave she approaches down the alley.

She reveals that she helped you because she knows that the men who were following you were men who belonged to a band of "freedom fighters" led by a tyrant named Griez. She despises their fight, since it is not for freedom, but oppression. They cause more harm than good in the city that she lives in.

One of the men that attacked you is not dead. When you question him he reveals that they had orders to kill you. Their information about who you are came from an unknown source. Now you have a problem. Your country is going to be attacked unless you can complete your mission, but even if you get home there is still a snake in the grass. Before you can return home you must find out who this unknown source is.

Your first order of business is to get all to the places that you have stored equipment and gather it all up. You are going to need every bit of help you can get. You take the gun from your attackers and head out armed with it and a wish of luck from the young woman. She might not agree with all the west's ideals, but she knows that what the "freedom fighters" are doing is not good either. She asks you as you leave if what you do is for peace or to fulfill orders. "We have killed Americans, Americans have killed us. Revenge ends nothing. Who will be the first to forgive?"

Now begins your grueling fight through the city. Until you get to your first equipment cache you must stay undetected. Your first equipment cache has been untouched. There you acquire an M-4 Rifle, Kevlar, and several ammunition clips. While there, you hear a tremendous explosion. It comes from what used to be your house. The whole city is thrown into turmoil. Stealth is mostly left behind. It's an all out brawl now.

At equipment cache two you gain access to communications equipment. You radio, on a channel that you know the Afghanis will intercept, that you were unable to get the information you needed, that your cover has been blown, and you are heading out. Of course, that's disinformation. After that it's off to equipment cache three.

It just so happens that this third cache has been found and looted. You are forced to find a gun runner or weapons dealer and steal what you need to complete your mission.

The assault on the weapons dealer's compound is not pretty. No one wants grenades exploding amongst boxes of ammo, or knocked over RPG's. Getting in and getting what you need without getting blown up on purpose or on accident almost makes you feel good to be out of the compounds confines and in the open.

The last cache you must visit is not something that will help you fight, but it will get you places that no gun will. Here you have stashed money, passports, and other personal belongings. This cache has been found, but left undisturbed, as a trap, in case you show up. A large force of men begin assaulting your location. Things are looking bad for you when a group of rebels comes to your aid. They have been wanting to throw off the reign of terror these "freedom fighters" have imposed, and now, with you, this one man army, tearing through the ranks of their oppressors, they are rising up to fight.

You must now fight your way out of the city so that you can get to the location of this terrorist meeting. After exiting the city you must drive through the desert. The drive is anything but a peaceful road trip. Bandits and sandstorms, and of course gratuitous artillery fire all combines to keep you on your toes. Of course it would be foolish to continue to drive through an extreme sand storm which is why it is fortunate that you find a terrorist training facility just when the storm is getting too vicious to travel through. You take shelter at the training facility and while you are there you decide you might as well take out a few of the bad guys to pass the time. You don't have to worry about them calling for back-up while the storm is raging. All communications are down. It turns out that this is the facility where Griez trains his men and bases his operations. As you shred your way through the facility you learn that it was a senator in America that sold you out.

After the storm clears you are able to make it to the next city, clean slate. No one knows you are there, all is quiet. You must take to the sewers and stealth to get into position to confirm that Hadiem is meeting with other leaders, and take them out. During that confirmation you learn that there is already a cell in Los Angeles preparing for the first wave of Hadiem's plan.

There is no way to quietly take out that many terrorists at once. To make sure you get them all it takes a big explosion which throws this city into action. You must fight your way to the airport and secure transportation out of hostile territory.

Of course the airport has been shut down by "freedom fighters." You must clear the way so that you can take a private jet. To do so you have to get from the terminal which has been cleared of all civilians, across the tarmac to the hangars, find the jet, prep it, and take off.

There is no way that you are going to be able to land at an airport without the proper clearance. If you try security will be all over you. To get to a passenger plane to the United States you are going to have to walk in as a civilian. You ditch the private jet and skydive down. You have to ditch all your weapons and walk into town as a civilian to get a flight back to America.

Once in LA it is your job to find the terrorist cell that will soon be learning of Hadiem's death. There is no telling where they will go or what they will do then. You catch up to them at a technology company that is developing alternative energy sources. You stop the destruction of the facility, and gather some very interesting information, but have one more stop before you can report back to base that you have accomplished your mission.

After all you've been through bypassing the senator's security system and staff should be a piece of cake. The politician is not at all pleased to see you.

When Traveler confronts the crooked politician he asks if the profit would do him any good when America fell. The politician sneers and narrates how America wouldn't fall. The attack on their homeland on a large scale would put America fully behind their efforts over seas. First Troops would be pulled back home to take care of the invasion, which would eliminate hundreds of terrorists, and then they could bomb the tar out of the countries where the attacks came from. You leave the senator with a copy of a file which shows that the senator was going to collect insurance money on the facility since its perceived value was in the billions and its destruction would have hid that it was really going bankrupt. You leave saying, "I can forgive you for trying to kill me, but you will face justice."

I even took a stab at some poetry now and again. Mostly it was inspired by the way Jonny Hart, the creator of the comic strip B.C. did things around the holidays.

The Day After Christmas

T'was the day after Christmas and all through the house
Every person had forgot what it's all about.

Their gifts they had opened with hardly a care
That God was the reason the season was there.

The child had been born a long time ago
Our Lord and Savior so His mercy we'd know.

And I in my sweatshirt and dad in his cap
Had tried so hard to remind them of that.

The Christmas without Christ, no cause to be merry
Without Christ our sins still we'd have to carry.

A family gathering is wonderful yes
Time to see family and friends that we miss
But gathering this day misses the why
The babe had to be born, to grow and to die.

A son to die because we are so lost
Seeking our own way just adds to the cost.

He gave us His son to care for
our need
He watched as His joy was nailed
to a tree.

Yet, we take His birth and wrap
it in lights
In trees and in presents and
partying nights
In songs about reindeer and
hoping it snows
The pain He must feel seems
nobody knows.

We give and we say, "See we give
cause He gave"
But none do our gifts, really
they save.

We have such a farce it's really
quite sick
Surrounded by idols of jolly
Saint Nick.

Idols they are
graven images all
Everywhere you look in streets
and in malls.

We raise up his picture and make
it his day
A made up character worshiped
this way.

Don't tell me it's just fun cause
that's just not the case
Christ's day has become one big
slap in His face.

I can't remember why I did this. It may have been sent as part of an application for a technical writing position.

PB&J: How to Make a Peanut Butter and Jelly Sandwich.

Peanut butter and jelly sandwiches are an easy, healthy, filling, and thoroughly enjoyable snack or meal component feasted upon by 4 out of 5 children each day.

If you have a knife and all three components of the PB&J: bread, seven grain is preferable for those concerned with health; peanut butter, smooth or crunchy; and jelly, any flavor will do and jam may be substituted for jelly, then you are ready to make your sandwich.

The standard PB&J is made from two pieces of bread with a layer of peanut butter and a layer of jelly between them. Start by opening the bread and removing two pieces. If you are not a fan of the crust I would suggest skipping the heel (first and last slices of bread in a loaf) and go for two regular slices. Place the stacked slices of bread on a plate or clean counter. Remove the top slice of bread from the bottom as if you were turning the page of a book. This will ensure that the completed sandwich will have a uniform exterior eliminating the mess of dripping peanut butter and jelly caused by an asymmetrical sandwich. Plus, you can laugh at your friends' frustration as they call you obsessive compulsive.

With the two slices of bread prepared go ahead and open the peanut butter. You may have to remove the safety seal under the cap if it is a brand new jar of peanut butter.

NOTE: It will help make the peanut butter easier to spread if you stir it in the jar a bit. Also there are natural peanut butters that separate and you will have to stir their oils back in.

Hold the jar over the left-hand slice of bread and scoop out whatever amount of peanut butter you desire. Just remember that the more peanut butter and/or jelly that you place on the sandwich the more of a mess it has the potential to create. Go ahead and set the jar down so that your hand is free to hold the bread while you spread the peanut butter evenly over the slice. You don't have to hold the bread, but it may be necessary if the peanut butter is cold or less creamy. Spread the peanut butter evenly over the slice of bread. Spread the peanut butter to within a quarter inch of the crust. Leave a little perimeter for squishage. Once you are done spreading the peanut butter wipe the excess off the sides of the knife on the inner rim of the jar to avoid getting peanut butter in your jelly. You may now close the jar of peanut butter. WARNING: If you have a relative who is allergic to peanuts, use a new knife to scoop and spread your jelly.

As with the peanut butter you may want to stir the jelly. Scoop some out onto the bread with your knife. Spread the jelly evenly over the bread leaving the same quarter inch perimeter.

Now that you have spread both the peanut butter and the jelly it is time to assemble the sandwich. Take the piece of bread on the left, the one with the peanut butter, and again like turning the page of a book, lay the slice, peanut butter side down, on top of the jellied bread. Jelly has a tendency to drip which is why you don't turn the jellied bread over onto the peanut buttered bread. That is also why you scoop and spread the peanut butter first; it has less tendency to contaminate the jelly. Apply enough pressure to secure the two pieces together. You will know you have used enough pressure when the peanut butter and jelly squish out to the crust. Your sandwich is now finished. Enjoy with a cold glass of milk.

Once you have mastered the basic PB&J you may want to go onto others like the Double Decker, and The Half. Mix multiple jellies or jams; the possibilities are endless. Remember to close the peanut butter and the jelly jars and wipe up any crumbs to keep the kitchen nice for your mother.

My first semester at Long Beach State I had taken Advanced Creative Writing and had gotten an A. Before registering for my final semester I went to see a counselor just to make sure that I wasn't missing anything. I was told that as an English: Creative Writing major I needed to have taken Intro to Creative Writing. Apparently my intro class from community college hadn't matriculated.

Introductory Creative Writing was taught by the same professor as Advanced. When I walked in the first day of class he looked at me and said, "What are you doing here. I gave you an A in advanced." When I told him the situation he asked if I wanted him to sign off on the class. I told him no, it would give me incentive to write. Best decision I ever made.

May First was inspired by my grandfather. It was one of the first things I ever wrote without having an idea of how it was going to end.

May First

The sun crept through the crack in the curtains and washed across Joseph's feet. Joseph was awake and remembering. He remembered how he used to stand at the edge of the sand and let the spent waves wash across his feet. He remembered that he always enjoyed just being at the beach.

Joseph began to pick at the haphazard scrap quilt that seemed to pin him to the bed. He was confused. He didn't know why this quilt was covering him. He didn't know whose it was, but it wasn't his.

Suddenly he lost interest in the quilt and began looking around the room. There were two plants in the room. Joseph remembered a woman who used to tend those plants.

"They need water, don't they?" Joseph spoke to the memory. When no one responded, he lost interest and went back to surveying the room. There were two tan chairs near the bed. He reached over and tapped on one and then nodded as if content that everything was the way it was supposed to be. Both of the chairs were worn and old, and reminded Joseph of a log. In fact, they reminded him of a driftwood log that he had sat on once when...

Joseph sneezed, and the thought drifted away. Joseph turned his attention to the room. He noticed that there were two plants in the room. One sat in a pot in the corner. It was a small, bushy tree-bush. The other plant was a fern on the dresser next to the bed. Joseph reached out and brushed the fern with his hand and smiled. The plant looked like it needed water.

Joseph realized that he was hot. The sun had crept up his legs like a rising tide warming the room. His eighty-eight-year old body got uncomfortable very easily. He pushed back the quilt that was draped over him. He wondered who had put it there. He knew he hadn't. Joseph closed his eyes and yawned. He didn't hear the door open, but a familiar slap slap slapping noise drew his attention. He opened his eyes to see a beautiful, white-haired woman carrying a pitcher of water walk across the room to the window. She set the pitcher down and opened the curtains, then the window. Fresh air rushed into the room and caused the woman's hair to stir.

Joseph smiled and watched the woman. She picked the pitcher up and walked over to the bush in the corner. She poured the water slowly into the pot and turned.

"Oh," she said catching Joseph watching her. "Nice to see you awake."

"Nice to..to..." Joseph chuckled as if he had said something profound. She didn't seem to get it. He gestured in the general direction of the plants. "They needed water?" he asked.

"Yes, they did," the woman answered with a smile. "How about you?"

"No, no. I've got about all the water I can handle." Joseph laughed at his own joke.

The woman walked across the room followed by the slapping sound. Joseph smiled stupidly at her. She leaned over and gave him a kiss on the forehead. Joseph's smile grew.

"What can I get you for breakfast?" the woman asked.

"Not hungry," Joseph said.

"Ok, maybe later," the woman said.

The woman turned and walked out of the room carrying the empty pitcher and the slapping noise followed. Joseph looked down and saw that the noise came from the woman's feet, or more precisely what she wore on her feet. Old leather thongs slapped against the woman's heels as she strode across the fresh white carpet.

When the woman left the room Joseph went back to looking around. He noticed two chairs that were a sandy brown and looked quite comfortable. They looked as if they had seen years and years of use. Joseph decided the two plants in the room must have been watered recently because the earth in their pots was damp.

Joseph's attention was drawn away from the chairs when a woman wearing a white flower-print dress walked in the room accompanied by the slap of thongs. Joseph noticed that her long white hair moved easily about her face and she was very pretty. She moved one of the chairs closer to the bed. Joseph wondered if she was the one who took care of the plants.

"Who are you?" Joseph asked.

"Who are you?" the woman asked smiling, yet there seemed to also be a hint of sadness in her voice.

"Joe.. Joseph. Joseph Mc Donald." Joseph said triumphantly.

"And I am Mrs. Mc Donald," the woman said. "That means I am...?"

Joseph seemed to think for a moment.

"Ashley." The word sprang from Joseph's mouth.

"That's me," the woman, Ashley said.

"That's you," Joseph said.

The woman held a small Dixie cup with many different colored pills in it.

"It's time to take your pills, Mr. Mc Donald," Ashley said.

"It's time."

Joseph yawned while he spoke. The wind tossed the curtains. They folded over in a shape that whispered back into Joseph's memory. His eyes seemed to clear and something seemed to come alive inside of him...

It's time. I woke up minutes before my alarm clock went off. I shut my eyes and tried to get a few more minutes of sleep, but my older brother, Gary came into the room. I listened to him walk through my room to my dresser. He knew that I knew he was there, but that didn't stop him. I heard the CD player switch on and in a few seconds "VS. The World" by Amon Amarth shredded through the silent morning. Black Metal before sunrise, quite a wakeup call.

"Let's go Little Man," my brother said.

"Ughh," I groaned. Without getting up I began blindly groping around the floor for my wetsuit. My hand landed on the familiar neoprene just when I was about to give up and actually get up.

"Naw uh," my brother said, "we're trunkin' it today."

That got my attention. I was up instantly.

"No way. I totally forgot." I said.

"Way, May first at the spot dude. No suits or no surf that's the rule"

"Man," I groaned. "Who came up with that rule any way?"

"Tradition. Hurry up and get your stuff," my brother said as he left the room. I sat there for a few seconds gazing longingly at my wetsuit and listening to the music. I waited for just the right lyrics.

"Always charge, never bend."

That seemed fairly appropriate. I got up and grabbed my trunks, flipped off the stereo, and left my wetsuit, my wonderful, warmth-preserving wetsuit, lying in my room. I grabbed a banana and the rest of the carton of orange juice from the kitchen, and grabbed my backpack from the hall as I ran out of the house.

Gary was already outside strapping his board on top of his black '71 Nova. I tossed my backpack in the car and chugged the orange juice.

I tossed the empty carton in the trash can on the way to get my board from the garage. Gary had the car running and the radio blaring. He was impatient, and I could feel my own anxiety rising.

"Hurry up," Gary said. He rapped on the roof of his car impatiently. I got my board strapped to the car rack in record time and we were off.

We sped through town and I had to smile. I was usually rushing down this road trying to get to school on time, and here I was almost at school two and a half hours early.

Gary pulled into the empty parking lot and kept the car running.

"Make it quick," he said.

I jogged through the empty outdoor halls to my English class. I duct-taped a large manila envelope with my term paper to the door and split. I got back to the car and we were pulling out of the lot just as the first teacher was pulling in. Gary spun the tires on the way out and we both howled.

Fifteen minutes later we parked along the road in a small dirt lot. From there we would have to hike about a mile to the beach, but that was cool. This was our secret spot and nobody surfed here. Well, not nobody and it wasn't that secret, but it was our spot. We had discovered it so we were given priority status anytime we surfed there. Everyone knew to leave enough space for the Nova to park beside the pepper tree at the edge of the lot.

We had just gotten all our stuff from the car when Casey's red jeep pulled up next to us. The soft top was missing and Casey stood and leaned over the roll bar with her camera.

"Smile boys, I'm topless." I couldn't help laughing as Casey snapped the picture. The flash was obnoxious.

Casey was the local photo genius. She had already gotten some pictures published. She was also hot, and Gary's girlfriend. "The morning warriors," she said. "Definitely a good title for that picture."

"Morning Case," I said

"Morning Joey," she said. Casey was seriously bubbly for five forty-five in the morning, but she was about the only one that didn't call me by my nickname so it was ok. "How ya doin'?"

"Stoked. Don't keep him too long," I said making kissing noises. I dodged a kick from Gary which was quite a feat considering I had a back pack on and my board in my arms.

I threaded my way along the scant path. Being one of the first trail blazers of the path I knew every rock and root that could trip me up so the dark didn't bother me. I could walk the trail half asleep if I had to. I had on occasion.

As I neared the beach my heart began to beat faster. I topped the hill and stopped between two piles of rocks. The waves breaking and the white water rolling in told me there were definitely waves out there. I rummaged through my backpack and grabbed my sharpie. I found a smooth rock and tagged it with J M and added it to the small pile along the left side of the path.

That was another part of our yearly tradition. No wetsuits, no checking the surf report, and first one to the top of the hill added a rock to the left pile. This was the first J M there, with a bunch of G M's. I looked at the large pile to the right of the path. Everyone would leave a rock there when they left. I didn't know then that it would eventually become a wall that bordered the path to our favorite surfing spot, that it would become a monument to every May first at our spot. Thousands of rocks for thousands of surfers. Years later it would be mentioned in an article in "Surfing" magazine.

I made my way down to the beach. The sand was cool under my feet, but once the sun was up that wouldn't last long. I set my stuff down by a driftwood log and stretched. I had a few minutes alone where the only sound was the crash of the waves and the beat of my heart.

The sky was beginning to lighten when Gary and Casey made their way onto the beach. They were tailed by Tom and Jerry - Thomas and Gerald Garcia.

"All right boys and girls," Gary got everyone's attention. "Joey you're the first one here. Give us a blessing." We all bowed our heads in silence.

"Carpe Undam." I said. "Seize the Wave."

"Fer sure!" Jerry said.

We threw fresh coats of wax on our boards and headed for the water. Casey clicked away with her camera.

I was surprised when the first water that lapped over my foot was warm. I took three running steps and launched myself into the water to begin the paddle out. I hated this part and I loved it. I was a very lazy surfer. There was nothing I wanted more than a friend with a jet-ski so I could be towed out to the lineup, but in reality I wouldn't have missed the fight to get out. I just like to complain.

A wall of white water came tumbling towards me and I dove. I got dragged back a bit and fought forward. I was forced to duck dive three more times before I got past the impact zone. I sat up and looked around. I was the first one out to the line up. Gary surfaced behind a wave and paddled over to me.

"You're growing up Little Man."

"Naw, you're just growing old," I said.

Tom and Jerry laughed at that as they came paddling over.

"All right. Seems to be your day. You take the first wave," Gary challenged me.

Tom and Jerry "Oooo'ed" and snickered.

I scanned the horizon and picked my wave. I paddled into position as the water gathered behind me. I could hear Gary, Tom, and Jerry hollering at me. I paddled hard and began sliding forward. This was the part I loved. There is that instant where the wave has you and it drives you forward. This must have been what it felt like for Superman to fly.

I jumped up and sailed down the face of the wave. I took a bottom turn to the left. I was more comfortable going left, being goofy footed, and I didn't want to screw up the first wave of the day. I watched the wave as I flew along. It was about head high. After a few quick turns I had to pump to beat a section, nailed a short floater then pulled out and paddled back to the line up. The first glints of sun began to dance on the water.

The guys were clapping and shouting.

"Looking good, Little Man," said a girl's voice from behind me. I turned to see Stacy come paddling out into the sunlight. I smiled.

"Yow," Jerry cat-called at Stacy. She did look good in a bikini.

"Was that the first wave of the day?" Stacy asked.

"Indeed," I said.

"You did us proud Little Man," she said. I ran my hand back through my hair to clear my eyes and waited for my next wave.

Within half an hour of my first ride most of the regs were there. Barry "The Flash" Goodman, Lightfoot - his real name was Brad, but no one, not even his parents called him that - and old man Whittaker in his kayak. I saw Casey talking to a small group on the shore. She pointed to the hill and I knew she was explaining the rules to them. The two guys in the group nodded, pulled off their wetsuits, and paddled out. The girl stayed there with Casey.

I caught another wave, actually I snaked it from Gary. It was about to close out so I shot down the wave gathering momentum, made the bottom turn, and shot back up the face and caught air. I made my way back to the lineup in time to hear Gary introducing everyone to the newcomers.

"... and that snake right there, is my brother" he said pointing at me, "Little Man."

"Joey," I said. I recognized one of the guys. Andy Underwood. He was in my Driver's Ed class. He had failed the class the first time he took it.

For a while everyone sat there waiting for the next set. Andy paddled for a small wave, only about chest high, and got to his feet. He was so shaky and unsteady that I was sure he was going to bail. Amazingly he rode the wave until it closed out.

A few sets later I had a primo wave. I had paddled to the far right of everyone and was in the right place when a monster peak showed up on the outside. I dragged my takeoff and managed to get in a fairly nice barrel for a few seconds. That's when Andy tried to drop in on the wave. He snaked me, but it's no biggie. He was just a beginner. I had to cut back to avoid him and I ended up getting thrown. I grabbed as much of a breath as I could before going under and instinctively covered my head.

The water tossed and turned me which was usually quite fun. I was enjoying the underwater ride when there was a tug on my ankle and then nothing. I kicked for the surface and looked around. My leash had pulled loose and I was about thirty feet from my board. I started to swim towards it when I was hit by a second wave. That wave took my board all the way to the beach. I resigned myself to the long swim to shore and tried to body surf in as much as possible.

By the time I reached the beach I was tired. I grabbed my board and decided to take a break and hydrate.

"Enjoy your swim?" Casey laughed at me. I ignored her. I set my board down and rummaged through my back pack until I found my bottle of water. I downed half of it instantly. I sat on the log and continued sipping my water and watching everyone else surf. I heard this slapping noise approaching so I turned. There was this radiant girl wearing a flowery swimsuit and sarong standing there smiling at me. Her sandals had made the slapping noise that caught my attention. It was her that held it.

Smiling at me?

Her long blonde hair was caught by a quick gust of wind. She reached up and brushed it back and I was enchanted. It was such a simple, unconscious move and it tossed me for a loop way worse than any wave had.

"Hi," she said.

"Uh, hi," I said. I moved over to give her a spot to sit on the log. She sat and I waited trying frantically to figure out something to break the ice. Something that wouldn't sound lame.

"I'm Ashley. You're Joey, right?" she asked. "Aren't you in Mrs. Hathaway's fifth period Biology class?"

"Yeah," I said. I felt like a moron. I must have sounded like a monosyllabic Neanderthal to her.

"Ok, this is going to sound kind of lame, but I asked my brother to bring me along so that I could ask you out without the whole school being around," she said in a rush.

"Oh," I said. I stared at her. She blushed. "I would love to go out some time." I said. That was all it took and I was in love...

"And I have been ever since." Joseph said and smiled at Ashley. Joseph didn't see the tears in his wife's eyes. The cup of pills had long since spilled to the ground. She wiped her eyes on her dress when she bent over to pick up the pills and when she straightened she was all smiles.

"Well, clumsy me," Ashley said.

"Yeah," Joseph nodded.

"I had better get you some breakfast," she said as she looked at her watch.

Joseph watched Ashley get up out of the chair the color of a driftwood log and walk out of the room followed by a familiar slapping noise. He knew there was something important about that noise, but couldn't place it. Suddenly he noticed that there were two plants and two chairs in the room.

"They need water," Joseph said. He then closed his eyes and promptly fell asleep.

I don't remember when I had this idea. I was doing a lot of examining how I wrote things and realized I didn't do that much research. I thought of actually doing this... purely for research sake.

Escort

Parker examined himself in the mirror. He wasn't happy with what he saw but then he never was. He didn't like his hair and his nose was too long and French. He had on the nicest pair of jeans he owned. He hated slacks. They were for funerals and weddings. His shoes were generic Vans and the long-sleeve shirt was wrinkle free having been just taken out of the dryer.

He took a deep breath and let it out slowly. This whole thing could end so badly that he would never be able to show his face in town again. He thought about calling the whole thing off, but then he would imagine over and over how things could have gone.

Parker paced in the living room. It was almost seven o'clock. He was so used to being early for everything that waiting on other's made him nervous. Was he forgetting anything? He had already showered and brushed his teeth. All his clothes were clean and, and, and he had almost forgotten deodorant.

He darted to the bathroom and slapped some Old Spice under his arms, careful not to get any on his shirt. He heard the knock at the door, took a final look at himself in the mirror, and went to the front door. He was tall enough to see through the window at the top of the door the limo waiting in the street. He felt a moment of panic.

The neighbors had to see the limo. They had to be wondering what it was doing at his house. Sink or swim time.

Parker opened the door and was blown away. There was a smiling brunette poised in a form fitting red dress. Parker almost hoped the neighbors had seen her walk up to his door.

"Trevor Adams?" she asked.

"That would be me," Parker smiled back. He hoped she didn't hear the nervousness in his voice. Of course if she did there was no way she would show it. This was what she did. She was a pro.

The woman extended her hand. A small gold bracelet was the only ornamentation she had. Her nails were long, and glossy, but not colored.

"My name's Violet."

"Nice to meet you, Violet," Parker said. He took her hand in his. Briefly he thought about kissing it, that might have been something a Trevor would do, but then, he wasn't really a Trevor and settled for the handshake.

Violet was a beautiful woman. Parker thought she must have been about four years older than he was. He grabbed his coat from next to the door and stepped out.

"Shall we," he said extending his elbow for her to take. She giggled and threaded her arm through his.

"Thank you," she beamed at him.

"I, uh, hope the limo driver doesn't mind waiting here," Parker said. "The place I have in mind is two blocks away. Unless, of course, you don't want to walk?" He looked down at her red, strappy high-heel shoes. He had never seen a woman with such beautiful ankles.

"Not a problem," she said. "unless it's more than three hundred feet."

"Oh," Parker looked back at the limo.

Violet smiled.

"It was a joke. It's fine, really."

They both laughed, her easily, him relived.

"You know, I wouldn't expect that there would be any place for us to go here. This place is so..."

"Podunk." Parker said.

"Podunk?"

"You know. Kind of like out in the boonies, nothing to do, Podunk."

"I didn't mean to-"

"Oh, it doesn't bother me. That's the way it is."

They walked down First Street and turned left at the post office. Parker stole a glance at

Violet. She was looking around and seemed genuinely interested.

"If you don't mind my asking, where are we going?"

"Dinner," he said.

"Dinner?"

"Dinner."

They turned right at South Broadway and walked past the pizza place to Jacks.

Parker held the door for Violet.

"Dinner?" she asked again.

"Dinner."

Violet tried to suppress a smile as she walked past him into the restaurant. Parker cleared his throat and followed.

The place was full and they had to wait a few minutes to be seated. For the first time Parker noticed all the awards along the wall behind the single register. Several years in a row this place had won Best Breakfast and Best Value for your Dollar. The stained-glass chandeliers cast everything in hues of red and yellow giving the place an autumn feel.

They were seated in a booth at the back of the restaurant by a young man.

"Can I get you folks anything to drink tonight?" their host asked.

"Violet," Parker defered to her.

"Iced tea."

"Iced Tea, and for you?"

"Water please," Parker said.

"Iced tea and a water. I'll be right back."

Parker found himself staring at Violet. She looked around the restaurant and then focused on him. She gave him a knowing smile.

"Well, what do you think?" Parker asked.

Violet let out a little laugh.

"What do I think? I've been to nicer places, but I've also been to worse. For being in the middle of Podunk, USA I'd have to say it's not bad."

"You like that word don't you?"

"Podunk, yeah, it's descriptive in a vague sort of way."

The host placed their drinks on the table. His gaze lingered on Violet for a moment. If Violet

77

noticed she didn't show. Parker took a drink of water and then chuckled.

"What?" Violet asked.

"I was about to ask,' So what do you do?' and realized how stupid that would be. I mean, unless you have another job?"

"No, this is it."

"Do you enjoy it?" Parker asked.

"Sometimes." Violet said. "What about you?"

"I work at the school."

"Teacher."

"Aid. I help with the students with disabilities."

"Oh. Do you like it?"

Parker thought for a second.

"No, I can't say that I like it. I mean it would be great if there was no need for my job. It's hard sometimes. You are working with such young minds and then you realize that some of them are never going to be anything but what they are as a seven year old. Some that are less disabled than others will go on to lives, have jobs, get married and all that, but then there are some that will have to have someone holding their hand every day of their lives."

Parker and Violet looked at each other.

"Sorry. I didn't mean to..."

"No, I asked. Besides, what you are doing is a good thing."

The server arrived during the awkward silence and placed their menus on the table.

"I'm Trish and I'll be your server tonight. Can I get you guys any appetizers?"

"You want anything?" Parker asked.

Violet smiled.

"No thanks, I'm fine."

"I think we just need some time to look at the menu," Parker said.

Trish walked off and Parker watched Violet over the edge of his menu. Violet scanned the menu.

Her eyes darted across the pages pausing here and there to read the details of an item. She looked up at Parker. He smiled.

"I'm not really all that hungry," Violet said.

"You know what, neither am I," Parker said. "Why don't we just get dessert? The pies here are great."

Parker stood up and held out his hand to Violet.

"Where are we going?" she asked taking his hand.

"To go see what pies they have today."

Parker led her to a cylindrical glass case with seven different shelves all full of pies. There were strawberry pies blazing bright red, and banana-cream pies with the cream mounding up taller than the pie was wide and many other pies.

"Oh." Violet clapped her hands. Parker saw her eyes sparkle in the glass. "They have pecan pie. Is theirs good?"

"I don't know. I've never had it. A pie made out of a nut, sounds wrong to me." Parker said.

"Pecan pie is the best."

"Well then we'll get a slice," Parker said.

"What about you, what are you getting?"

"Trust me, one slice will be plenty."

They returned to their seats and waited for Trish to come back. Parker tried to think of something engaging to say, but everything he thought of seemed forced and trite. He was about to resort to one of those thoughts when Trish sidled up to the table.

"Are we ready?"

Violet looked at Parker.

"We have, through unanimous decision, decided on a slice of pecan pie."

"Well I wouldn't say unanimous," Violet said.

"Okay, she chose, I agreed."

"One slice of pecan pie." Trish said.

"And two glasses of milk," Violet said. "We can't forget the milk."

Trish headed for the pie case and pulled out a dark brown pecan pie. She placed a slice on a plate and brought it back to their table. Violet gasped at the size of the pie.

"That's a slice?"

Parker nodded.

"Told you one would be enough."

The slice of pie was about the size of a brick. A very syrupy, tasty-looking brick. Mounds of pecans the color of Violet's hair sitting atop sugary pecan goo shone darkly in the stained light. Parker doubted that a pie made of nuts could taste good, but it sure looked great.

Trish set two glasses of milk on the table and scurried off. Parker watched Violet stare at the slice of pie.

"That's a slice," Violet repeated.

"It could be worse," Parker said.

"What do you mean?"

Parker pointed to a booth on the opposite wall where Trish was delivering a mountainous yellow and white dessert.

"We could have gotten the banana-cream pie."

"That's a pie?" Violet asked. "It looks more like a Rose Parade float."

"Well there's not that much to do out in Podutia so we eat."

Parker picked up his fork.

"Would you do the honors?"

Violet shook her head. Her hair flicked about her face with the movement. Parker's pulse quickened. He had almost thought he was becoming comfortable with such an attractive woman and then she did something like that which made her even better looking.

"I think you should go first," Violet said. "After all this is your virgin pecan pie experience."

Parker tried not to blush. Of course she hadn't meant anything by that. Parker looked at her. Her face was completely innocent. There was no double entendre there, was there?

"Well, maybe you should go first so you can tell me if it's a good pecan pie of not. Keep me from forming any negative associations."

"No. This is something you need to go for without any preconceived notions."

Violet cut of a piece of the pie with her fork and held it out to him. The pie was like nothing Parker had expected. It was nutty, but it was sweet and soft and oh so good.

"Oh no," Parker said.

"What?"

"I think that I am going to get fat with a pie this dangerous being made so close to my house every day."

Violet giggled.

"You'll just have to start working out more." She took a bite of the pie and her eyes lit up. "Oh wow."

"I take it this is a good pecan pie."

Violet nodded as she chewed. When she had swallowed she said, "This is a great one."

They both dug into the pie. Parker remembered to keep his bites small, and not eat like a starving wolf. Sooner than he would have thought they were finished with the pie. Parker took care of the bill and sat back at their table.

"So, Trevor, what now?" Violet asked.

"That I don't know. My plan for this evening was simply to get some pie. Mission accomplished."

"Mission accomplished," she echoed.

"Mission accomplished."

Violet stood.

"Well then, I guess I should be getting back."

They meandered on their way back to Parker's house. Violet was very quiet and then she looked at Parker.

"You honestly hired me just to have a piece of pie with you didn't you?"

"Well, no."

Her expression didn't change, but the kindness went out of it.

"I have a confession to make. I didn't honestly hire you." Parker took a deep breath. "My name isn't Trevor Adams. I just, I wanted to be someone else for the night. I guess I am just like every other guy who hires an escort. Living out some kind of fantasy. I just wasn't comfortable being me, you know? I felt like having a friend around even if it was only a temporary friend. My real name is-"

"Parker!"

Parker and Violet looked to see the old Vietnamese lady that lived across the street from Parker waving at them.

"Parker Adams, don't you just look adorable. Who is this?"

Parker waved.

"Hi Mrs., Trinh. This is Violet she's..."
Parker looked at Violet.
"I'm Violet, one of Parker's friends," she said.

Parker breathed a sigh of relief. Violet really was good at her job. Now he wouldn't have to explain that he was hanging out with an escort. They walked up the walk to his house and Parker hung his head. He wished she hadn't said it though. It stung.

"I'm sorry that I lied to you."

Parker opened his door and stopped when Violet put her hand on his back. He turned and she smiled.

"I wasn't lying when I told Mrs. Trinh that I was your friend. So you wanted to be someone else, we all do at one time or another, but you were honest with me. I like honesty. And you really just wanted a dated for some pie," she handed him a card with her number on it, "so next time you want to hang out, don't call the agency, call me." She said as she walked away.

Parker looked at the card and smiled. There was no suggestion of anything beyond friendship and Parker was ok with that. He smiled completely relaxed for the first time that night."

"Hey Violet!"

She turned.

Thanks for sharing my virgin pecan pie experience with me."

Violet laughed.

"Thank you Tre- Parker," she said and laughed again.

I know it's sappy happy. I just didn't have the heart to give it a not-so-happy ending.

Solitude was a venture into the unfamiliar genre of horror and suspense. It was based largely on a nightmare I had. I enjoy nightmares. They haven't scared me since I was about seven. I remember two that really bothered me, but after those I started to be inspired by odd dreams. It was a lot of fun developing this into a cohesive piece.

Solitude

A rotten wind blew in from the ocean. It picked at the parched scrub grass and tossed the brittle, long-since dropped, leaves of a distant oak. A slate marine layer hid the sun leaving everything damp, but nourishing nothing. A pitted and cracked two-lane highway wended north and south along the coast.

Along this road a man backpacked his way north, alone. He wouldn't have called this stretch desolate, but it was. The cliffs and ocean to his left and the scrub hills to his right offered little in the way of majestic views. The same ocean and same hills languished under the same gray sky that he had hiked beneath since beginning this leg of his journey in the early morning.

Brian was used to the looks he'd receive in town during his treks. The locals thought he was a vagabond, a transient, he didn't belong. He didn't mind that. However the looks he had been given that morning had been different. They had been so... he didn't know what they had been so, but they had been it. He rubbed his neck, trying to relieve the tension he felt just thinking about those looks.

He wasn't out begging. He wasn't homeless or in need of money if that's what they thought. In fact, he had a nice apartment back in Long Beach and a job that he loved, in a city that was mostly bearable. That's why he was out backpacking along the coast, the city was mostly bearable. When the city became too much he would leave it all behind for a week or two and hike along lonely highways to refill what he saw as his own inner reserve of solitude. After that he could stomach another couple of months of city life.

He was on the fourth day of this trek and knew that it was going to be another long one. Work had been extra stressful. He had been the team leader for his company's new project. He had had his nose to the grindstone, as it were, up until the last possible minute. The constant phone calls from his team members, constant meetings, constant, constant, constant had stripped him of everything. He was tired. More than that, he hadn't had any alone time since the project began. It had taken him three days on the road just to begin to unwind.

The sound of a car driving north drew his attention. He was on the south-bound side of the road, walking against the flow of traffic, as any hiker knew you should. No seasoned hiker trusted a car to see a pedestrian or to stay on the road. Drivers had a nasty habit of seeing only other cars and veering toward pedestrians. On this road, that had been surprisingly a non-issue. This was the first car to pass him in hours. He turned and walked backwards. An older model Volkswagen Rabbit approached, slowing down.

The driver pulled to a stop, not bothering to pull off the road. He rolled his window down, and stuck his head out.

"You need a ride?" he called.

"No thanks," Brian said. "I'm hiking to get some alone time."

"Well you picked a helluva place to do that," the man said. "Course if you don't stop you should be able to make it to town with light left to spare. You're sure now?"

"I'm sure, but thanks."

Brian waved. The man took off rolling his window back up. Walking north again, Brian glanced out to sea. There, out on the water, a ray of sun had broken through and was shining down from the murk. It made for a dazzling display prompting him to pull out his camera and snap off a couple of photos. He crouched to get a shot of the light through the dead grass and saw what looked like a trail heading down the cliff.

He took the picture and then headed for the trail. The ocean had been beside him his whole trek, but the road had run along the top of the cliffs and he hadn't found any suitable way to get down. With any luck this would be more than a short animal trail ending in a tangle of shrubs a few feet off the road.

Brian worked his way along. From his vantage point up high it appeared the trail seemed to wind its way all the way down to a sandy cove below.

He took the trail, carefully picking his way down because the dirt was loose and the trail was small. One wrong step could send him down for sure. He watched his feet as much as the trail ahead which caused him to spot the bones. They were mostly buried along the edge of the trail. The skeleton was far from complete. It could have been anything. He took a quick series of pictures since this was the most interesting discovery he had made on this trip and continued down to the beach.

From up on the cliffs, the waves had looked like they were rolling lazily in, but as he got closer Brian could hear them crashing against the rocks. They were strong enough that he could taste the salt that was being thrown into the air by each collision with the rocks. As he made his way down two more rays of light broke through the clouds. One speared the water closer to the first, and the second illuminated the beach.

Finally the path opened up and leveled out. Brian found himself staring at a sight of raw earthen splendor. The sand was windswept clean though the air was dead calm. The breeze up on the cliffs failed to reach down to the beach. This beach had been left untouched since the last storm to hit the coast.

The sand was already starting to warm in the sun. Brian set his pack aside and took several moments to bask in the warmth. Out at sea the waves were rolling in overhead and crashing against the rocky reef. Large jagged outcroppings stuck out of the water like the arrowheads Brian had found on his last trek. Inside the reef knee high ripples reformed and washed ashore spending the last of the wave's energy.

He would have to remember this place. Brian had always wanted to learn how to surf. This looked like a great place to do it. He wouldn't want to chance the outside break, but inside the reef there was promise.

The grumbling of his stomach told him that it was probably close to noon. On these treks Brian took no watch and his phone, off and tucked into his cargo-pant pocket, was to be used in an emergency only. There was sun up and sun down and when his body told him to eat or sleep, and that was about it. A second grumble urged him to unpack a granola bar and an apple.

Sitting there enjoying the sun, crunching his food and watching the water, Brian could feel the solitude sink into his bones. This was what he had come out here to find. He finished the granola bar and tucked the wrapper into his bag. It would be sacrilegious to litter in a place such as this. He held his apple in his mouth while taking his shoes and socks off. He rolled his pants up and strolled to the water.

When the water washed over his feet Brian began to have second thoughts about surfing here. The water wasn't just cold; it was you-said-the-wrong-thing-at-the-wrong-time-to-your-girlfriend frigid. Even with the sun pouring down on him Brian felt chilled. He lingered there while finishing his apple. By the time he got to the core his toes had fallen numb. He tossed the core out to sea. It wasn't littering. It was returning nature to nature as he saw it. In a few days the core would be gone, unlike a wrapper or Styrofoam cup.

Meandering back to his pack Brian took his shirt off. He dug sunscreen out of his pack and armored his body with it. His girlfriend was always trying to get him to wear sunscreen. Breanna was a fiend for the stuff. She would put it on if she were going to be out in the sun for ten minutes. She had forced him to bring some SPF 80 along with him. He had yet to use it. She would know if he hadn't even if his tan had faded by the time she got back from her trip to Europe because the tube would be full. Brian had thought of squirting some out, but his conscience just wouldn't let him.

He laid his shirt out on the sand and propped his head up on his back pack, shut his eyes, and listened to the waves. The swell was dying but too slowly for Brian to notice. Each set of waves rolled in with less power than the one before. Brian was lulled by the rhythm and after a few minutes he dozed off. Once, a fly landed on his nose causing him to stir and roll over onto his side. Half an hour slipped by. An hour, then another half. Slowly Brian opened his eyes.

He was burned but not as badly as he could have been. The sun had lowered below one of the cliff arms of the cove and for the last half hour Brian had been shaded. He felt relaxed after his nap, ready to continue his trek.

Brian gathered his things, shod his feet, and found the trail leading back up the cliffs. The climb was more difficult than he had expected. The way down is always easier than the way up. The loose earth tended to slide out from under him and for every three feet he managed forward he slid one back. By the time he reached the place where he had found the bones Brian needed a break. Catching his breath Brian wondered if he should take one of the bones as a souvenir. He thought better about it and decided to just let them lie. Who knew what disease the animal might have died of. There could be germs lurking in the bones just waiting for a new host.

It had taken Brian just over twice as long to climb the trail as to descend it. It was probably well past four now. Much of the marine layer was gone and the parched grass was vivid in the afternoon sun. The ocean had taken on a happy blue hue and despite being sun burnt, Brian felt wonderful. He began walking north again, with the sun slowly sinking on his left casting shadows as the day wore on.

The road began to climb uphill. It turned away from the cliffs and curved around a hill that had been too steep to build the road over. From around the bend Brian could hear a car coming. It sped by, and Brian was confident, relying on his innate L.A. radar, that the driver had been going at least sixty in a posted thirty-five zone.

He's looking to get himself killed, Brian thought. If the driver lost control of the car for even a moment he could be over the side of the cliffs. Brian pictured the car smashing into the rocky reef.

"Would serve him right," Brian said. L.A. freeways were one thing, but speeding along narrow, sea-side cliff roads was just stupid.

As the sun sank the air took on a chill. The hill blocked the light. Brian moved over to the other side of the road to stay in the sun. It was worth it for the warmth even if he now had oncoming traffic at his back. One car an hour didn't seem like too big of a danger. At the apex of the curve Brian found himself shadowed even on the far side of the road. When he emerged on the other side the sun was blinding and warmer than he had remembered, and there was a hint of something else.

It was a strange sensation. It was as if he had lost something more than just light in the shadow. It reminded him how he had felt when he had left the town, left the strange, stranger-looks behind.

Brian found that he was breathing heavier. He had increased his pace while in the shadow and only slowed when he was again in the sun. He hadn't consciously done it, it was just that it was getting colder and he wanted to spend as much time in the sun as he could. That must have been it. Up ahead the road curved away from the cliffs again.

He stepped off the road to take a leak. He was zipping up when he noticed another skeleton. This one was definitely a possum. It was also completely intact. Brian took several pictures of the skeletal possum. Its jaw hung open as if it had died snarling, and amazingly the scavengers of the area had picked it immaculately clean without dislodging any of the bones.

At the next bend Brian stopped and pulled his sweater out of his back pack. He had to shake a bit of sand out of it before pulling it over his head. The sweater cut the chill and he smiled. He picked up his pack and even started to whistle going around the next hill.

This hill extended a long distance eastward. It was steep like the trail that led to the beach, but not extremely high. Brian decided that he would climb over it instead of walking all the way around. The Earth was loose here as well. Again, it was not as bad as the trail, but it made for treacherous footing.

A small landslide caused Brian to fall to his hands and knees. He barely stopped himself from face planting in the ground. He found himself staring at the skeleton of a snake. To his amazement there was a skeleton of a mouse inside it; the snake had died while digesting the mouse. His wonder was cut short by a stinging in his hand. Brian turned his palm up to see a sliver of rock embedded in his hand. With a grimace he pulled it out and was about to toss it aside when he took a closer look. It wasn't rock, it was bone. Brian looked to where his hand had landed and saw the crushed remains of a lizard's skeleton.

"What the..."

Traversing the last few feet Brian stood, sucking on his cut, gazing north. He had to shade his eyes against the wan sunlight. Ahead he could see the road wound around another hill, stayed straight for a mile or two, and then ducked into a valley before entering a small town.

Brian looked down and saw the bones of what looked to be two or three animals strewn about the hill top. Standing there alone gave Brian a sickly feeling. He made his way down the hill quickly and set a quick pace down the road. A half hour later he was just starting to go around the final hill. Along the road he had seen more animal skeletons and suspected that the white patches among the field grass were not piles of sun-bleached sticks.

The shadows had grown in length and were beginning to deepen in shade. As Brian rounded the bend he saw a thin fog that was beginning to gather in the chill darkness. At the apex of the curve the fog spanned the entire road. Brian was almost there when he heard a car approaching. The squeal of tires was all Brian needed to hear. He moved as far off the road as he could.

He still had to dive out of the way as the car came screaming around the bend out of control. It slid sideways for just a moment, until the driver cross steered and rocked violently as his car regained traction and sped off sucking the mist with it. Brian picked himself up and ran shouting after the car. If the driver heard him he didn't stop and was soon around the bend. Brian heard the squeal of tires once more and ran again in case the car had hit something. Brian was mad, but wanted to be able to help the driver if need be.

There was no crash and the sound of the car's motor soon faded in the distance. Brian's moment of concern was scattered as the mist had been. What a jerk, almost hits me, can barely control his car.

The wisps of mist that the car had kicked up began to settle back together. The road behind Brian was choked with it, but he was too upset at the driver to notice. Brian trekked on around the bend and back into the sun. The sun was swollen and orange now. The light it cast was still warming to the soul, but offered little in the way of comfort to the body.

In the distance Brian could see the town. He saw the car roll into town and thought, great, maybe I can find that guy and... and what. Brian had never been a tough guy. It might be nice to at least glare at the guy in the bar though, if he was there. Brian glared ahead, practicing for the upcoming confrontation. While he was glaring about he saw that on the lee side of the hills more mist was forming. He didn't think it was that cold, but then he was more of an inland guy and the coast seemed to have its own weather patterns.

Brian walked on. As he neared the town he could see that it was rather small and far from prosperous. The driver probably hadn't even stopped there. Of course, it took thriving business to grow a town and what was there for business out here? Brian looked at the hilly fields again. They must be used for grazing or at least had been. The barbed wire fence looked intact as far as Brian could see.

One single rose bush had grown up from a ditch along the barbed wire, and a single white rose had bloomed upon it. Forgetting about the driver and town, Brian took out his camera. If he could get in the right position he could get the rose, backlit by the fading sun.

Brian crouched next to the fence. He brought the rose into focus. The sun wasn't positioned where he wanted it so he leaned a little. He found himself leaning against the wire of the fence. The picture was almost perfect. He leaned a little more. One of the barbs dug into his shoulder. Almost there. He pushed a little more and then he had what he wanted.

In his viewfinder the orange of the sun washed over the rose so that it faded from white to orange. He clicked off four quick shots before the pain in his shoulder became unbearable. Then he eased up and shot another few pictures of the rose just white. Brian rubbed his shoulder where the barb has stuck him. He looked down to see he was ever-so-slightly bleeding. The prick stung, but it had been worth it for the shot. It might even be worth entering in a competition. Flowers were always the money shots. Looking past his shoulder in thought, his eyes focused on the ground just on the other side of the fence.

Bones. Very large bones. They were too large to be a possum or even mountain lion. Then he noticed the skull. Large hollow orbits set high on the elongated skull stared out at nothing. A horse skull. As majestic and awing as horses are alive Brian felt that their insides, when laid bare, were eerie. Brian took a quick photo and looked around.

All was calm, and all was quiet. He thought he could just hear the sound of the waves though he was two miles inland. It must have been his imagination. Down at the bottom of the ditch a thin tendril of mist had formed and drifted lazily. Brian hopped back to the other side and almost fell. He could have sworn that when he jumped the mist had tried to follow him. He had been distracted and twisted his ankle when he landed.

Brian limped back from the ditch. It had to have been his imagination. Loose gravel crunched under his feet and he found himself in the middle of the road. Behind him the shadow almost reached his feet and there was mist there too, a larger patch. It seemed to surge against the light like the waves against the reef. Brian hobbled toward

91

the town. It had to have been the wind caused by his jump, that's all.

Still, Brian found himself walking a circuitous path to avoid shadows, especially those that happened to have mist in them, as more and more did. Every time he put weight on his ankle it jolted his leg. Brian was pretty sure that this trek was done. Unless, he could ice the ankle in a hotel room in the town and have it heal enough by tomorrow, but after playing soccer in high school he tended to know when he would be laid up for a few days. This was one of those times.

Above him an eagle screamed and dove into the field. It swooped and rose with a snake clutched in its talons. Brian stopped and reached for his camera. The eagle lost its grip and the snake plummeted. It landed just off the road dispersing a small cloud of mist. Then, quickly, violently, the mist plunged down upon the snake. Brian almost dropped his camera. He stared as the mist swirled around the snake. The snake hissed which then turned into something else. Was the snake screaming? The sound gained in intensity and then faded away. The mist swirled and rolled in upon itself and then drifted away. All that was left was a clean, white skeleton of a snake, mouth agape, and fangs poised.

Brian took a deep breath. He hadn't realized that he hadn't been breathing. He knew that it had been him screaming, not the snake. He shook his head in disbelief and looked around. There were several pools of mist now. They were forming in the weaker shadows, places where the light slipped by seemed to sprout a gray tendril as soon as the light was gone.

Panic tore into Brian; the sun was just slipping over the horizon. But, there was the town. Several lights were on. He began to run. Every time his right leg took his weight he wanted to scream. The ankle was ablaze now. Once, twice he almost stumbled. Once, he almost fell headlong into a shadow where the mist seemed to rear up and boil in anticipation. Ahead the town loomed. It was all that he could see.

Brian cried as he ran. He looked at the sun, now halfway gone. And then he was there. Not at the town, but the small valley before it. There in the darkness the mist circled reaching further outward as the sun died. There was no way to cross. Brian wailed in despair. Then he remembered the car that had passed through the mist earlier.

He dropped his back pack and pulled off his sweater. He descended into the valley swinging the sweater in front of himself, fanning a path. Down into the valley he surged, cutting a clear swath. Before he could hope he was climbing the other side. Tears of pain mingled with tears of relief as he crested the top.

Brian gave a cry of relief which died as the last rays of the sun vanished from sight. All around the mist was coalescing, and it was coming for him. Brian ran. The town was so close. He heard a snap and wondered what it was. Two strides later he knew. He tumbled headlong in agony. He must have fractured his ankle earlier and the running on it widened the fracture until it had just given out. In his already pain-filled frenzy the break hadn't even registered.

"Help me!" he called.

He tried to crawl forward, scraping his hands and knees, but the mist surrounded him. He waved his sweater at it, weakly keeping it at bay, praying that someone would come help him. A thin finger of mist reached for his legs and he batted it away. Behind him others gathered.

One wrapped around his throat and Brian felt the dampness scraping across his skin. He flailed in vain as more mist poured over him. He opened his mouth to scream and the mist poured down his throat killing the sound.

The mist swirled and boiled and then drifted on, leaving a fresh skeleton clutching a damp sweater. Above, an eagle circled once more and then winged its way south, to warmer hunting grounds.

This was another piece done for class at Long Beach. At the time I was re-evaluating the way that I looked at Martial Arts and wanted to put some of that philosophy into a story. What surprised me was that it even came out in the form of the prose itself, a long, meandering, artsy beginning and an abrupt ending.

Beautiful Art, Brutal Craft

This was the closest to dancing I would come. I couldn't see myself, but I had been told that it was, not to brag, awesome. I know that to me watching someone do a form, someone who was good, was like watching a dance. They made you see the opponents they were fighting. I hoped others could see the creatures I was fighting. I was picturing seven-foot-tall, gorilla-like creatures as my opponents.

The thought dissipated almost instantly. As I moved through the Kata, I was focused, but not oblivious. I saw people watching me. I heard the sound of a car alarm go off in the parking lot. I felt sweat slide down my temples and between my shoulder blades. I perceived all of it but focused on none of it. The only sound that mattered was the snap of my Gi signifying that I had proper speed and power on my punches and kicks. The only sights that mattered were the opponents that I imagined in front of me and to the sides. The only feeling that I paid attention to was my balance and the strength in my stances. Any thought or sensation that wasn't critical to my execution of the form was gone before I completed the next move.

"Eyah!"

"Eeeep!"

I couldn't help grinning when one of the watchers was startled by my Kiai. I guess they had gotten used to the beginning student's timid battle cries. I had lost that self consciousness years ago and was able to roar.

Step-Block-Punch-Block-Kick-Step-Finish

I bowed and took several deep breaths while standing at attention.

"Good, very good. You were letting your hands drift when you threw your last kicks. Otherwise, good job Sempai. Take a seat."

"Yes Sensei," I said.

I bowed and turned to take my seat with the rest of the class lined up against the wall. As I moved back to my spot I glanced at my girlfriend and saw her beaming. I smiled back before turning and kneeling.

After all the students had performed a Kata I was called up again. It was time for sparring. For the first round I faced one of the higher ranking students. We squared off. I rocked my head popping my neck. He clenched his fists cracking his knuckles. On Sensei's signal we became whirling dervishes. It was nice to not have anyone else on the mat with us. After the two minute mock fight I was hyped.

"Good," Sensei said. "Sempai Cody sit. Rokyu Eric up."

Now I found myself facing the dojo's newest blue belt.

"Now Sempai," Sensei said addressing me, "You are facing someone at a much lower level. I want you to react appropriately."

"Yes Sensei," I said.

While I sparred with Eric I looked for openings that I could have exploited, but instead of instantly attacking I hesitated and attacked at a speed that pushed Eric, but didn't dominate. This was actually harder than sparring with someone at my level. After two agonizingly slow minutes Sensei ordered us to stop.

"Rokyu take a seat. Ikyu Josh, up!"

I was going to fight for another two minutes. I began to wonder what Sensei was trying to teach me.

Josh outranked me, but I'm a better fighter than him. I don't say that to brag. It's just a fact. After training for so long you begin to gauge others. Josh had to work hard and practice endlessly; to me it just came natural. He had to go through a Kata over and over to get it to stay in his head. Two runs-through was all it ever took me to have it memorized. After two minutes I was breathing hard, but not as hard as I should have been.

After Josh sat down I was paired with another beginning student. Ryann, my girlfriend. We bowed and took our ready stances. She preferred to fight in a side horse, almost traditional. I favored something of a cross between a cat stance, and a natural stance. She, like most beginners, fought with her hands clenched in tight fists. It's a mistake because keeping your muscles tight drains energy and slows your movements. When I fought I preferred to hold my hands in an almost Muay Thai style, hands open, palms down and arms slightly extended as if I were appealing to my adversary to calm down. Ryann's eyes locked with mine for a second and then she looked away.

Look at me. Look at me.

"Begin." Sensei's curt command sent us into motion.

Kick-move-punch-move-block-kick-point scored. Ryann grimaced. I waited for her next attack.

Avoid-avoid-redirect-move-block-punch-point scored. Ryann hissed and shook her head.

"Watch my eyes," I whispered. Ryann looked up into my eyes and I attacked.

Kick-avoid-punch-kick-knee-block-block-duck-sidestep-kick-avoid-block-punch-move-kick-point scored.

Why did you quit watching my eyes? You were doing so well, I thought.

Two minutes later Sensei stood.

"Good job Ryann," he said. "Take a seat."

I glanced at the clock. There were only three minutes left before the end of class.

"Sempai, face me. Rei."

I bowed to sensei. Now there was no time for any thought critical or otherwise. There was only reaction.

Blockavoidsidestep-punchkickblock-blockduckblock-sidestepkickkickkickkneeblock-backstep. Sensei tripped up my foot and sent me falling back. I rolled instinctively and got my feet under me just in time to see Sensei coming at me. Internally I growled at myself for my mistake.

Crouchsidestepkick-sidestepblockpunch-punchpunchblock-avoidblock-avoidavoidavoidblock.

97

On and on and on. Two minutes later I think I can remember hitting Sensei once. How many times had he hit me?

More than twenty.

"Yame," Sensei called the sparring to an end. We bowed and Sensei motioned for the class to stand for closing. We closed class customarily. I then turned to Josh.

"Nice roundhouse," I said, referring back to our sparring match.

"Yeah, thanks," he said, "but I saw you back off instead of taking that opening I gave you on accident. I was wide open."

"I felt like being nice," I said. I glanced over my shoulder just in time to see Ryann walking out the door. "I'll be right back."

Outside the wind chilled my bare feet and sweaty body as I jogged to catch Ryann. I wished I were one of those monks that could meditate in the snow for hours.

"Ryann."

She turned when I called her name.

"Hey," she said distantly.

"You did real well tonight," I said trying to draw her out of her mood.

"Yeah right," she said. "You hit me so many times. I think I may have got you once."

"It happens. You were doing really great until you quit watching my eyes, but that's something everyone, even me, needs to work on. It's no biggie. I have been doing this so much longer than you. Don't get hard on yourself."

"I know," she said.

"So you're going home.?." I asked or stated. It came out in such a way that even I couldn't tell if it was a question or not.

"Yeah," she said.

"Why don't you stay for a while," I invited.

"I feel weird hanging here. I don't really know anybody, but you and your brother, and it's weird because he is Sensei."

"Well, if you stay you can get to know some of the other students," I said.

"No, I'd rather just go home," she said.

"Can I see you later?"

"Yeah," Ryann said. "Come over when you are done here. I'm just going to go home, shower and read."

"Want to go out," I asked. "It's been a while."

"We'll see," she said.

I gave her a quick kiss and watched her drive away. Then I jogged back to the Dojo just in time to be challenged to a grappling match which I accepted.

Forty-five minutes worth of grappling later I was totally exhausted. Time flies when you are kickin' butt. I drove home breaking a fair share of traffic laws. I was in a hurry to get a shower and go see Ryann. As I drove I sketched a plan in my head. A bonfire at the beach seemed like a good idea. By the time I got home I had the rest of a romantic night planned out.

When I got home the house was empty, which was good. No one would want to talk to me and take up my valuable time. I was pulling my Gi top off before I was in the house. I tossed it on the floor along with the rest of my dirty clothes for that week.

I'll do laundry tomorrow. I don't have time right now, I though.

I turned on the water for a hot shower and brushed my teeth while I waited for the hot water to reach my bathroom. Just before hopping in the shower I flexed in front of the mirror trying to look menacing. I failed miserably.

My shower must have broken records because I was in and out before the mirrors had a chance to start fogging up. I scrambled around my room as I toweled off, trying to find some nice, clean clothes. I remembered that my brother had thrown a load of laundry in the dryer before leaving for the Dojo, so I darted through the living room to the garage. I grabbed a pair of pants and headed back to my room.

I got a quick laugh imagining my brother walking in with his girlfriend to see me darting around the house naked, drying my hair, and carrying a pair of pants.

On a whim I grabbed some graham crackers and milk as filler to keep my stomach from rumbling. I dressed while I snacked and managed to avoid getting any food on my clothes. The last thing I did before leaving the house was brush my teeth again. I wouldn't want to give Ryann a graham cracker-kiss.

One quick stop at the store for flowers and I was on my way. Ryann lived on the outskirts of town along a seldom used road so I felt fairly comfortable breaking the speed limit by fifteen miles an hour.

When I pulled up Ryann's long driveway I wasn't surprised to see two vehicles that didn't belong to the family parked haphazardly wherever they could fit. The black F-150 was Ryann's sister's boyfriend's and the Red Saturn I had never seen before. As I approached the house I could hear plenty of laughing going on in the kitchen. I knocked before opening the door even though I had been told numerous times to just enter.

I poked my head into the kitchen from the empty living room. Ryann, her sister Theresa, Theresa's boyfriend, and a girl I had never seen before were scattered across the room all talking and laughing.

Theresa yelled my name when she saw me. She jumped off her stool, ran over and gave me a hug and a bright smile. I smiled back, even though I felt a little odd. Theresa retreated to her boyfriend and Ryann replaced her at my side. I handed her the flowers and she smiled. She gave me a quick kiss, a familiar kiss, which wasn't like her to do in front of everyone. I knew something was going on.

"This is C.J," Ryann said. The other girl nodded.

"Hi," I said.

"She is Theresa's friend from like the cradle" Ryann chattered.

"Cool," I said.

"She moved to Arizona like four years ago."

"Oh," I said.

"We were just catching up on old times and I know you wanted to go out tonight, but I thought we could just hang here."

Suddenly I was hurt and angry. I tried to keep it out of my voice. I think I kept my face pretty blank.

"That's cool," I said. "I'll just see you later."

"You could hang with us?" Ryann pleaded.

"Naw, I need to get out," I said, "I've been too cooped up lately. It was nice meeting you C.J."

"I'll walk you out."

"Ok," I said.

Ryann took my arm and we left the house. She was oddly being extra clingy. We got to the edge of the large cedar porch before anyone spoke.

"Are you mad?"

"Yes," I said.

"Why?"

"More hurt than angry," I said.

"Why?"

"Because I have seen you for maybe two minutes outside of class in the last two weeks," I said.

"---"

"Then you shelve me for your sister's friend. I don't know how long she is here, but last month I cut out on my cousins, that I haven't seen for years, who were only here for one day because you really wanted to see that movie. You said that it might not be in theaters the next day and you just had to see it in the theater. I took you. Look I don't want to fight and I don't want to ruin your time with her-"

"Then stay," Ryann said.

"Why?" I asked.

"It'll be fun."

"Ryann what am I going to do? Sit there and listen to you guys reminisce. I'd be just a bump on a log."

"But-"

"Look, it's ok," I lied.

"You could-"

"No," I said. "Just have a good time, I'll see you later." I turned and walked to my car. I heard Ryann call my name and ignored it. I ignored her reflection in my rearview mirror, watching as I drove away.

I found myself driving randomly around town. I was ignoring speed limits, hoping that the miles would eat up my anger. I hadn't thought about where I was going and found myself in front of the

Horse Head Lounge. I decided a little pool wouldn't be a bad idea.

I had hung out at the Horse Head every once in a while since I was fourteen. The sign in the window said you must be eighteen to enter, but it was understood that was just for show. Everyone brought their underage brother or sister over the years.

I was already upset, and walking in to hear "I Did It All For The Nookie" blaring out of the juke box just irritated me further. I went over and searched through all the crap for something more to my taste. It took me a full three minutes to find "Hells Bells", "Iron Man", and "Fade To Black." As I finished with my selection the next song came on. Bon Jovi began whining about how he just wants to live while he's alive. I tried to shut it out.

I was walking back to the bar to pay for a table when I saw a group of women out of the corner of my eye. Naturally I scoped them out. I crushed any feeling of guilt I should have had, besides who says you can't still look at the menu once you've ordered. My attention was on the blonde in the group lining up her shot rather than where I was headed and I bumped into someone. I turned to see that I had messed up the shot of an unruly character, who was with three other unruly characters.

None of these guys had less than three tattoos, and none of them looked like they weighed less than one hundred and eighty pounds.

"Watch it freak!" the guy growled.

"Sorry," I said though frankly I was in no mood to apologize to anyone for anything.

"Well that's a start," this mammoth grunted, "but you messed up this game, so you are going to pay for our next game."

"No," I said flatly.

"What did you say!" he roared drawing just about everyone's attention instantly.

"I said," I said, "that I am not going to pay for your game. I apologized and that is the only thing you are going to get." I knew I was pushing his buttons, but by now I didn't even care. There was a bit more verbal sparring, but I don't remember what was said. I was watching him closely so I saw him tense for what he thought would be a sucker punch.

He threw a punch at my head. It was a wide arcing haymaker that is typically thrown by someone who has no real conception of how to fight. I could have hit him twice before his punch hit me, but then it would look like I physically started the fight. I merely avoided the punch and waited. He would either decide it wasn't worth the effort or try to hit me again or go for it. He tried to hit me again. This time I fought back.

After avoiding the punch I counter attacked in a way he never expected. I stepped straight at him and broke his nose with a rising elbow. He reeled back and I followed. I jumped up as I grabbed his head and slammed it into my knee. He fell to the ground unconscious and bleeding. This whole exchange took about two seconds, but I was breathing harder than I had after two minutes of sparring.

One of this guy's braver buddies decided to help his friend. He swung at me with a pool cue. I stepped back out of range. He swung a few times and I stayed back getting my timing. After his fourth swing I stepped in while he was following through. He tried to hit me with a quick backhanded swing, but I expected that. I blocked the cue with my forearm. Let me make this clear. That hurt like heck, but I'd rather get hit in the arm than the head any day. Besides, pain is fifty percent mental. I kicked him in the groin causing him to bend over. I kicked his face causing him to straighten. I punched him three times in the face causing him to stagger.

I knew this guy was done, all it would take is a small shove to put him on his back, but I didn't want to fight anyone else so I went for the gusto. A jumping, spinning, crescent kick to this guys head while he was standing straight up looked very intimidating. Good thing no one there knew that it was one of those all-for-show-not-very-practical moves. I landed as he hit the ground, and I waited.

I tried to look menacing and at the same time nonchalant, as if I didn't care if anyone else wanted to fight. It may have worked. There were no takers. Now I felt weird. I hadn't really ever been in a fight, and didn't know what to do. I apologized to the bar tender and made myself scarce.

Most of my longest pieces have been scripts. The screenwriting class that I took at Allan Hancock College got me hooked. I liked the format. I liked getting a story out without feeling obligated to hose down my audience with blatant description.

The Limit was an idea that sprang into my head while I was skating through town. I had passed a couple of bars and was wishing that a bar could be used for something constructive. I then had to sit down at a bus stop and scribble furiously as ideas hit me. Every time I was about to get up and continue to skate another idea had to be jotted down.

A lot was written with continuation in mind. I wanted to set myself up with as many possibilities for the future as I could. For some I left things really open ended such as the identity of the drug dealer. There are several ways that he can be tied in or snipped out, but never settled on one. The first episode didn't require it, nor would there be much left hanging if he never returned.

The Limit

EXT THE LIMIT BAR - NIGHT

The neon-red words "The Limit" cast a tainted red glow on the building and surrounding street. The tail-lights of arriving motorcycles merge with the glow. The noise from inside the bar enlivens the night.

INT THE LIMIT

Truck drivers, bikers and biker chicks, and the occasional straggler crowd the bar. A mostly ignored band plays slightly rock country in a corner.

Behind the bar, RILEY GRANT, a smoke-aged, alcohol-preserved, thick shouldered man takes a bottle from the back shelf and casually smacks the butt of a co-ed bartender young enough to be his daughter.

The bartender squeaks. The men at the bar chuckle. Riley leaves the bar to join DAVY, who is just as smoke and alcohol treated but with more facial hair, at a table.

                    DAVY
     Rye, breakin' out the good stuff.

Riley pours two tumblers full.

                    RILEY
     Every now and then.

                    DAVY
     More like every day.

Both men laugh. They raise their glasses together and drink.

                    DAVY
     Ah, that hit the spot.

To their left a very young, very drunk woman tries to coax her boyfriend onto the small dance floor. Riley and Davy turn to appreciate her every move.

                    DAVY
     'Member when we were young like
     that?

Riley contemplates his glass.

                    RILEY
     Nope, and with a few more shots,
     neither will you.

They both laugh again.

                    DAVY
     Shoot, if he won't dance with her,
     I will.

Davy gets up and approaches the woman. He half
dances up to her. She gives her boyfriend a last
look, smiles at Davy, and they dance.

Several guys around the woman's boyfriend make cat
calls and jokes, egging the boy on. Finally he
steps out and cuts in. Davy bows to the couple
slightly and rejoins Riley.

                    DAVY
          Still warms the heart.

                    RILEY
          That's just the liquor taking
          effect.

                    DAVY
          Hey, you know who that kid looks
          like? Little Nicky. Where is your
          boy anyway?

                    RILEY
          Not exactly sure. Got a letter or
          two a couple years back, but
          that's about it.

Another guy tries to cut in on the woman and her
boyfriend. It desolves into a fight that spreads.

                    DAVY
          'Member when we were young like
          that.

Both men down their drinks, get up, and get
involved in the brawl.

EXT THE LIMIT - LATER

The neon lettering flickers off. The last patrons
of the bar trickle out. Holding a condensation-
coated beer to his eye, Davy exits with Riley
last. Riley locks the door.

107

                    RILEY
            That youngster sure had a mean
            right cross.

                    DAVY
            You noticed that while you were
            taking those uppercuts.

Riley slaps his belly.

                    RILEY
            With all this padding I barely
            felt them.

Riley snags the beer from Davy as they walk toward
their motorcycles. He pops it, takes a drink, and
hands it back to Davy. A few steps later, Riley
clutches at his side and stumbles.

                    DAVY
            Thought you said you didn't feel
            'em.

Riley falls to his knees and then on his face.
Davy drops the beer and rolls Riley over.

                    DAVY
            Rye, what's wrong? Rye!

Riley gasps a few times, grasping at Davy's vest,
before his eyes shut and he goes limp.

INT PARTY - NIGHT

People laughing, chatting, flirting, and everyone
drinking. Everyone except NICHOLAS GRANT. Nick
passes by a group of people and grabs BOB's
shoulder.

                    NICK
            Hey Bobby, it's been fun, but it's
            past my bed time.

                              BOB
                    I don't know if I should let you
                    drive home man. Being all tanked
                    like that.

The girls give the guys a weird look. Nick waves
and takes off.

                              BOB
                    He doesn't drink.

                              GIRL
                    How come?

                              BOB
                    He hates it and he has early
                    mornings.

                              GIRL
                    What does he do?

EXT BEACH - MORNING

Foamy white-water surges over the sand and then
retreats back to the sea. Nick treads onto the wet
sand and examines the ocean. He switches his
surfboard from one arm to another and pulls at the
shoulder of his wetsuit.

The water is empty as far as the eye can see.
NOoone wants to be out this early for ankle-biting
shore break.

                              NICK
                    Welcome to the Pacific Lake.

Nick zips up the back of his wetsuit, jumps in the
water, paddles out, and does his best to rip up
the mini waves.

EXT GROCERY STORE - LATER

A bus pulls to a stop on the street. Nick exits
carrying his surfboard and wetsuit.

INT GROCERY STORE EMPLOYEE ROOM

Nick sets his surfboard in the corner, pulls a trash bag out from under the sink, and stores his wetsuit in it. He clocks in, grabs a work apron off a hook, and heads out.

INT GROCERY STORE OFFICE - LATER

EMILY answers the ringing phone.

> EMILY
> So Cal Fresh, this is Emily speaking.... Uh huh.... I see, one moment please.

Emily puts the phone down and leaves her office.

INT GROCERY STORE PRODUCE SECTION

Nick and an elderly lady are in the middle of a discussion.

> NICK
> Most people will steam them longer, but I like asparagus to have just a bit of a crunch. Go ahead and try it at eight minutes. Leave the water on the stove. If you don't like it you can always steam them longer.

Emily approaches. The old lady sees her before Nick does.

> OLD LADY
> Emie dear, you hire the nicest young men.

> EMILY
> Thank you ma'am.
>   (MORE)

                    EMILY (CONT'D)
          I'm sorry to say that I have to
          pull this one away from you. Nick,
          there's a call you need to take in
          my office. It's a lawyer.

Nick gives the old lady a conspiratorial look.

                    NICK
          See, I'm not really all that nice.
          I need a lawyer to keep the police
          off my back.

The old lady giggles, pats Nick on the cheek, and
wanders off. Nick enters the office and takes the
call. Emily watches his reaction from outside.
Nick listens, nods, says a few words, and then
hangs up.

Emily waits for Nick to come out. After hanging up
the phone he puts both hands on the desk and leans
against it. After exhaling a deep breath, he comes
out.

                    EMILY
          Everything okay?

                    NICK
          My father died last night.

                    EMILY
          I'm so sorry.

                    NICK
          Don't be. Um, I'm going to need
          some time off. I have to fly out
          to Indiana and take care of some
          things.

                    EMILY
          Go right ahead.

INT CAR RENTAL AGENCY - THE NEXT DAY

Nick has a backpack and is standing at the counter.

              CLERK
     What brings you to Indiana, Mr.
     Grant?

              NICK
     Death in the family.

              CLERK
     Oh, sorry to hear it.

              NICK
     It happens.

              CLERK
     Death and taxes. Well, what kind
     of car would you like?

              NICK
     Whatever's the least expensive;
     I'm kind of on a budget.

              CLERK
     Not a problem. Here you go, and as
     a small gesture I'm going to go
     ahead and waive all mileage fees
     and only charge you for one day.

              NICK
     Thanks a lot.

EXT HIGHWAY 31 - LATER

Nick opens the hood of the car and steam billows out.

              NICK
     Thanks a lot.

An eighteen-wheeler barrels past causing the steam to fly about. Behind his car a motorcycle pulls off the road. RACHELLE shakes out her hair as she pulls her helmet off. Nick shuts the hood.

                    RACHELLE
          You look like you could use some
          help.

                    NICK
          It's been doing this all day. I
          get a few miles and then the car
          needs to rest. We'll make it
          eventually.

                    RACHELLE
          Where are you headed?

                    NICK
          Mount Ayr.

                    RACHELLE
          I'd hate to leave you stranded.
          You should follow me, if your car
          will start. These back roads can
          get a little tricky.

                    NICK
          No kidding.

                    RACHELLE
          Yeah, so try to keep up.

                    NICK
          Well it just so happens that I got
          the rental agencies last incognito
          drifter. Looks like a beater,
          tears up the street.

                    RACHELLE
          Right. I'll keep it under sixty-
          five.

                    NICK
          How about fifty-five. Last time I
          checked Vader steam from a car
          isn't a good thing.

EXT MOUNT AYR - LATER

Rachelle rides to the edge of town with Nick
clinging to her. She pulls up to the curb and
pulls off her helmet while Nick dismounts.

                    RACHELLE
          Here you are, safe and sound.

                    NICK
          Safe maybe, but sound may be
          pushing it, especially after that
          last hill. Thanks for the ride
          though.

                    RACHELLE
          Don't mention it. I can't believe
          your engine actually blew up.

                    NICK
          That's because I paid extra for
          the rental agencies "Run Into a
          Cute Girl on a Motorcycle Plan."

                    RACHELLE
          Oh, what's that?

                    NICK
          You get a button that allows you
          to blow the engine so you have an
          excuse to ride with the girl on
          the motorcycle.

                    RACHELLE
          So what if she just leaves you
          stranded in the middle of nowhere?

                    NICK
          It's a gamble. You never know with
          strangers. Speaking of, I'm Nick.

                    RACHELLE
          Rachelle. Go see Jake, at Jake's
          Towing. He's got a great mechanic.
          I have to get to work. Once you
          get that straightened out you
          should come by Greensleeves.

                    NICK
          Just might. Thanks.

Rachelle rides off.

INT MORTUARY - LATER

Two alabaster angel statues and a few flowers are
all the decoration in the lobby. Somber organ
music is barely audible. As Nick examines one of
the statues, MR. D enters from the side door.

                    MR. D
          Can I help you?

                    NICK
          I'm here to take care of funeral
          arrangements for my father.

                    MR. D
          The name of the deceased?

                    NICK
          Riley Grant.

                    MR. D
          Ah, you must be Nicholas. I've
          been expecting you.

                    NICK
          Sorry to keep you waiting. I had
          some car trouble.

                    MR. D
          Not what you need at a time like
          this. I'm sorry for your loss.

                    NICK
          I guess I'd better get used to
          hearing that, huh? I just want to
          get this over with.

                    MR. D
          Ah, I see. Why don't we step into
          my office?

INT GREENSLEEVES CAFE - LATER

Behind the counter TIFFANY reads a book. The
friendly neighborhood old man, ELI, snores away in
a cushioned corner seat.

Rachelle enters. Tiffany looks up. Rachelle grabs
an apron and checks the cream container on the
counter.

                    TIFFANY
          You're late.

                    RACHELLE
          I stopped to pick up a cute,
          stranded guy.

                    TIFFANY
          You picked up a stranger?

                    RACHELLE
          He's not a stranger. I got his
          name... after I gave him a ride.

                    TIFFANY
          Please God, don't let that be a
          euphemism. Do you still remember
          his name?

                         RACHELLE
               Nick. This scrumptious boy's name
               was Nick.

                         TIFFANY
               Nick? His last name wasn't Grant,
               was it?

                         RACHELLE
               He didn't say. Why, do you know
               him?

                         TIFFANY
               I thought I did, if it's him.

                         RACHELLE
               That's a drama-filled statement if
               I ever heard one.

Tiffany stuffs her book into a backpack.

                         TIFFANY
               Can I borrow your bike?

Rachelle tosses the keys to Tiffany.

                         RACHELLE
               He never said where he was going.

                         TIFFANY
               If it's who I think, then I know
               where he's going.

                         RACHELLE
               Hey, I called dibs on him. Oh, and
               put some gas in the tank this
               time, will you?

EXT MOUNT AYR MORTUARY - LATER

Tiffany pulls up on the motorcycle.

INT MOUNT AYR MORTUARY

Tiffany enters and heads for the office. She pokes her head in on Mr. D doing some paperwork.

                   MR. D
        Can I help you?

                  TIFFANY
        Is Nicholas Grant here?

                  MR. D
        I'm sorry miss. He left a while
        ago.

                  TIFFANY
        Did he say where he was going?

Mr. D shakes his head.

EXT MOUNT AYR MORTUARY

Tiffany stands next to the motorcycle. A gust of wind swirls leaves around her feet. It sparks a memory. She jumps on the motorcycle and tears off.

EXT HILLSIDE - LATER

Tiffany clambers toward a large tree at the top of the hill. Up in the tree Nick sits, eyes closed, breathing quietly.

                  TIFFANY
        Still climbing trees, huh?

                  NICK
        Looks like.

There's an awkward silence between them.

                  NICK
        There used to be two trees up
        here.

                    TIFFANY
          There was a party which led to a
          fire. A couple of kids got hurt.
          People stopped coming up here. I
          haven't climbed up here since...
          years ago.

                    NICK
          So why now?

                    TIFFANY
          I heard you were in town.

                    NICK
          I forgot how fast word travels in
          small towns.

                    TIFFANY
          That's just how us small town
          yokels are.

                    NICK
          You know I didn't mean that.

                    TIFFANY
          Will you climb down now?

                    NICK
          You could always climb up?

Another silence. Tiffany puts her hands on her
hips.

                    TIFFANY
          I could always cut this tree down,
          but one Grant is enough for this
          month.

Nick climbs down. Nick drops the last few feet.
Tiffany steps up to him, slaps him, and throws her
arms around him.

                    TIFFANY
          Oh, God, I've missed you.

                    NICK
          I've... missed you too.

Nick buries his face in her hair. They share an
intense hug. After a while they separate.

                    TIFFANY
          Where did you go? Where have you
          been?

                    NICK
          At first I wandered around picking
          up odd jobs. Eventually I made my
          way to California. Even went to
          school.

                    TIFFANY
          How could you just... I mean I
          understand, kind of, but you
          never...

                    BEN (O.C.)
          Hey guys!

Ben comes jogging up the last few feet of the
hill. His hands are tucked behind his back.

                    BEN
          I heard Tiffany was speeding in
          this direction. The scuttlebutt is
          flying. I figured...

Ben brings his hands out from behind his back. He
holds out two pieces of cardboard.

                    BEN
          Huh? Huh?

                    TIFFANY
          Ben, I don't think that-

EXT BOTTOM OF THE HILL - MOMENTS LATER

Ben and Nick are surfing down the grassy hillside on the pieces of cardboard. Tiffany tromps down the hill behind them.
Near the bottom Ben eats it and tumbles down the rest of the hill. Nick comes to a stop next to him. Both guys are laughing. Ben jumps to his feet and hugs Nick.

          BEN
Good to see you man. I mean, I'm sorry about your old man, but it's good to see you.

          NICK
It's good to see you, too.

Tiffany clomps to a stop next to them.

          TIFFANY
You two are just a bunch of kids.

          BEN
Never grow old. Come on Tiffany, take a ride.

          TIFFANY
No thanks.

          NICK
Don't knock it till you've tried it.

Ben takes the cardboard to a few kids playing at the base of the hill. They take the cardboard and go running to the top.

          BEN
Well this is seriously pushing my ten minute break. We'll catch up, right?

                              NICK
                    Sure.

                              BEN
                    Bye guys. Again Nick, I'm sorry
                    about your dad.

Ben takes off.

                              NICK
                    I still have some stuff to take
                    care of.

                              TIFFANY
                    I'm here if you need anything.

                              NICK
                    I know. You always have been.

They hug again.

Nick walks off.

                              TIFFANY
                    I'll be there tomorrow.

EXT MOUNT AYR MORTUARY - NEXT DAY

Starkly dressed mourners file into the building
beneath a bright shining sun.

INT MORTUARY

Mourners pass by the open coffin giving their last
respects to Riley. Nick stands by the coffin. The
mourners offer him their condolences. Tiffany and
Rachelle enter and take seats in the back.

INT MORTUARY - LATER

Davy is at the podium finishing his speech.

                    DAVY
          Riley was the kind of guy you
          wanted next to you in a bar fight
          or in a fishin' boat. Here's to
          you Rye.

Scattered applause and murmurs rise as Davy takes
his seat and the PASTOR steps up.

                    PASTOR
          Now, as the Lord has said, let us
          have the son honor the father.
          Nicholas Grant.

Nick slowly takes the podium. He scans the room.
Many people nod and smile.

                    NICK
          You have all been trying to
          console me in my loss, but I feel
          that maybe it should be me
          consoling you. You have lost more
          than I have. My father... many of
          you knew him, were his friends,
          even loved him. I see your grief
          and expectation and wish I could
          meet it with uplifting words, but
          I can't. What I remember about my
          father... he was a drunk and he
          wasn't there. Some father's are
          not there because they are working
          hard to provide for their
          families, not him. I remember too
          many nights where my dinner was
          leftover nachos, sometimes soggy
          with beer, and a couple handfuls
          of mixed nuts. Where your memories
          of my father are of good times I
          remember him at home, passed out,
          half-naked on the living room
          floor. I remember childhood
          discoveries like learning that I
          could tell by the smell what
          someone was drinking.
                    (MORE)

                    NICK (CONT'D)
          I know this funeral is supposed to
          be about remembering and honoring
          my father, but I can't. Not right
          now. Maybe someday but not today.

The assembly is aghast. Nick leaves the podium and
walks straight out of the building followed by
disbelieving stares and angry murmurs. Mr. D takes
the podium.

                    MR.D
          Excuse me, ladies and gentlemen.
          Now would be... I mean... we will
          now proceed to the cemetery for
          the burial.

EXT MORTUARY - MOMENTS LATER

People are exiting the mortuary as the casket is
loaded into the hearse. Nick is walking away.

EXT CEMETERY - LATER

The casket is lowered into the ground as the
Pastor speaks. Nick is not there.

                    PASTOR
          From the dust we were taken and to
          it we return. Lord, today we lay
          this man, husband, father to rest.
          Embrace him in your loving arms.
          Amen.

The crowd whispers "amen" and disperses.

INT RESTAURANT - LATER

Nick eats alone. BRADY and DYLAN enter, spot Nick,
and storm over to loom above him.

                    BRADY
          You have a hell of a nerve!

                    DYLAN
          Uncle Riley deserved better than
          that.

                    BRADY
          What do you got to say for
          yourself?

                    NICK
          Nothing more than I already said.
          What I said was true, every word
          of it. He was closer to you
          cousins than he ever was to me.
          You even smell like him, cheap
          whiskey at eleven in the morning.

Brady knocks Nick to the floor with a monster
punch. Nick stays down. Tiffany runs into the
restaurant.

                    BRADY
          I'll kill you!

                    TIFFANY
          Hey! Back off!

Tiffany steps between Brady and Nick. Nick gets to
his feet.

                    TIFFANY
          You guys are family, for God's
          sake.

                    BRADY
          No family of mine would talk like
          that about his kin at a funeral.
          No family of mine.

Brady and Dylan tramp out of the restaurant. Nick
sits back down at his table. Tiffany sits across
from him. She takes a few pieces of ice out of his
water, wraps them in a napkin, and holds it out to
him.

                         TIFFANY
               Jeez, Nick, are you okay?

                          NICK
               Asks the first person who hit
               me... I'm fine.

                         TIFFANY
               What did you expect? I don't even
               like Brady, but I can see why he'd
               be ticked. Your dad was a big name
               around here. So you didn't want to
               praise him, that's fine. You could
               have said a few ambiguous words
               and been done.

                          NICK
               But it wouldn't have been right.

                         TIFFANY
               What's that supposed to mean?

                          NICK
               You don't know why I left, do you?

                         TIFFANY
               No. I thought that maybe your
               father was beating you and you
               just had to leave after your mom's
               accident.

                          NICK
               Beating me would have meant that
               my father paid enough attention to
               notice I was there.

                         TIFFANY
               So why did you leave?

Nick's watch BEEPS.

                              NICK
                    I have to go. I have to be there
                    for the reading of the will.

INT LAWYER'S OFFICE - LATER

Nick enters to the glares of Brady, Dylan, Davy,
and several other if-not-hostile-then-indifferent
looks from BARRY GILES, RANDAL MEYERS.

The seats are taken up by Brady and Davy. Everyone
else is crowded around the office and no one
offers to move, so Nick shuts the door and leans
against it.

                              LAWYER
                    Now that we are all here, we may
                    begin. You are all here because
                    you were mentioned in the will.

The lawyer pulls a stack of papers out of a manila
folder on his desk and begins reading.

                              LAWYER
                    The Last Will and Testament of
                    Riley James Grant. First, to my
                    nephews, I will the entirety of my
                    savings account.

He pulls another paper out of the folder.

                              LAWYER
                    And that is a total amount of
                    eleven thousand, seven hundred
                    dollars.

Brady and Dylan turn to each other and smile.

                              LAWYER
                    To Davy Jones I will my
                    motorcycle, my military
                    paraphernalia, and my baseball
                    card collection.
                              (MORE)

                    LAWYER (CONT'D)
          To Tammy Baylor, who my assistant
          Randal Meyers is sitting in for
          since she could not be present, I
          leave my fishing boat, trailer,
          rods, and tackle. To Barry Giles I
          leave my house, and to my son,
          Nicolas Grant, I leave The Limit
          and all that is in and on the
          land.

He puts the paper back in the folder.

                    LAWYER
          That's all there is. Brady, Dylan,
          we'll make an appointment to go to
          the bank and either switch over
          the account or withdraw the funds.
          Barry, here is the key to the
          house, and I believe that Mr.
          Jones has a key to Mr. Grant's
          motorcycle. Oh, yes, Mr. Grant.
          The title and keys to The Limit.

The lawyer takes the title and keys out of his folder and hands them to Nick.

INT CAFE - LATER

Rachelle is at the counter. Nick walks in and takes a seat in the corner. Rachelle scampers into the back room, fixing her hair as she goes.

INT BACKROOM

Tiffany is adding up receipts. Rachelle stops to look at herself in a mirror hung on the wall.

                    RACHELLE
          He's here.

                    TIFFANY
          Who?

                    RACHELLE
          Your friend, Nick. How do I look?

                    TIFFANY
          Jeez, Shell. He just buried his
          dad today. I don't think this is
          the time for...

Tiffany makes a "whatever" gesture.

                    RACHELLE
          From his eulogy, I don't think
          he's all that heartbroken, and if
          he is, then he could use some
          distraction.

                    TIFFANY
          I guess it's a good thing you're
          on the clock right now. Why don't
          you get back to work, and let me
          talk to him?

Tiffany and Rachelle exit the back room. Rachelle
slips behind the counter, Tiffany takes a seat
across from Nick. Nick is studying the deed to The
Limit.

                    TIFFANY
          How'd it go?

                    NICK
          Not sure. It was my first will
          reading.

                    TIFFANY
          How are you?

                    NICK
          Brady and Dylan got all the money
          so that should keep them in good
          spirits for a while. I think I'm
          safe, unless they spend it on good
          spirits.

TIFFANY
That's not what I meant. No matter how you thought you felt about him, you just lost your dad.

NICK
Father. I lost my father, not my dad.

TIFFANY
Dad, father, whatever. Changing the word doesn't change what and who he was.

NICK
Exactly. Calling him a dad doesn't make him something he wasn't. Without him I wouldn't be here, that's true. He fathered me, but that's it. After that it was like I wasn't there.

TIFFANY
How can you say that? I remember when you went fishing with him.

NICK
He took me, once, after I begged him. I hooked my finger baiting my hook... he fished for two hours while I sat there with a hook in my finger.

TIFFANY
That's why you never went with my dad and me?

NICK
Anytime I thought of fishing all I could think about was that hook in my finger and my father, popping open another beer between casts.

                    TIFFANY
          If I would have known I never
          would have...

                    NICK
          It's okay. Come on, I want to show
          you something.

EXT THE LIMIT - AFTERNOON

Nick and Tiffany stand examining the bar in the
afternoon light.

                    NICK
          This is my family legacy, a bar. I
          wouldn't be surprised if there
          were back taxes owed on the
          business, building, or the land.

                    TIFFANY
          Oh, God, Nick, I just realized,
          how is your mother going to get
          medical care? Your father's
          insurance is going to be gone.
          What happens to her now?

                    NICK
          I'm not sure. I've been paying the
          monthly dues for her insurance
          policy for years.

                    TIFFANY
          I didn't know that. I thought your
          father just couldn't let her go.
          She's been in the coma for so
          long.

                    NICK
          Oh, he was willing to let her go,
          but I wouldn't let it happen. Not
          and just have him forget.
                         (MORE)

                                                  131

                    NICK (CONT'D)
          The thing is the policy has almost
          reached the extent of its
          benefits. I'll have to find a way
          to pay the bills. I could sell The
          Limit or tear it down and sell the
          land.

                    TIFFANY
          And then what? You'll have some
          money, but what are you going to
          do? Your mother wouldn't want you
          to put yourself on the street to
          keep her semi-alive for one more
          month. Tear it down and you will
          only waste what you have been
          given. Your father's gone now. As
          hard as it may be to hear, maybe
          it is time to let your mom go,
          too.

Nick and Tiffany walk around the bar. There is a
car parked halfway behind the building. Two
teenagers crowd around the driver's side door. The
driver is handing them a baggie through the
unrolled window.

                    NICK
          Hey, what's going on?

The kids bolt, dropping the baggie. The driver
peels out and drives off. Nick picks up the
baggie. Nick opens the baggie and dumps out the
white powder.

                    NICK
          How long has this been going on?

                    TIFFANY
          The last couple of years the drug
          problem has gotten worse around
          here.
                         (MORE)

                    TIFFANY (CONT'D)
          It used to be that the worst that
          went on was the high school
          football team dismantling some
          poor farmer's tractor and putting
          it together on the roof of his
          barn. No it's this.

INT THE LIMIT

The light from outside flits through the shutters.
Nick opens the shutters fully. Stains and
imperfections that the night hides are revealed in
the daylight. Tiffany takes a seat in one of the
booths.

Nick slowly circles the main room of the bar. He
takes in all the pictures on the wall, many of
them are of his father and a smiling friend
fishing, hunting, motorcycling, drinking.

                    DAVY (O.C.)
          Many memories in here.

Nick turns. Davy is standing in the doorway. He
walks from the door to the bar and runs his hand
along it.

                    DAVY
          Some great times.

Nick walks around behind the bar. He sets the key
to the place on the bar.

                    DAVY
          For a lot of folks.

                    NICK
          Rowdy times?

                    DAVY
          Some of the best.
                    (MORE)

                    DAVY (CONT'D)
          I remember one time, your dad and
          Tommy Rourke got into it bad. A
          band had their stuff set up and
          your dad ends up taking Tommy's
          head and slamming it into one of
          the cymbals. Everyone went dead
          silent for a moment. Then everyone
          in the bar was laughing their
          heads off, even Tommy. They ended
          up drinking the night away.

                    NICK
          People get hurt?

                    DAVY
          Now and then. 'S like anything
          else.

Nick takes down a shot glass and a bottle off the
shelf.

                    DAVY
          Heh, that's the bottle your father
          used to win bets. He'd bet a
          stranger that he could drain any
          bottle in the place. He made sure
          that that bottle was always the
          fullest.

                    NICK
          I remember, with water.

Nick pours a shot glass full and pushes it across
the bar to Davy.

                    NICK
          Have a drink, Davy. It's on the
          house.

                    DAVY
          That's just water.

134

                    NICK
          I know.

                    DAVY
          If you're trying to say something
          just say it plain. We all know you
          can, real plain.

Nick reaches up above the back shelves and takes
down the liquor license. He places it on the bar
and carefully folds it into a paper airplane. Nick
holds his creation up for a second and then flicks
it across the room and out the door.

                    NICK
          Plain enough for you? This is my
          place now and we are closed till I
          say so.

Davy shakes his head and stands.

                    DAVY
          You're some kind of piece of work,
          you know that?

Davy walks out of the bar. Tiffany slips out of
the booth and takes Davy's spot across the bar
from Nick.

                    TIFFANY
          Do you know what you are doing?

                    NICK
          There are some things that I need
          to take care of.

                    TIFFANY
          Does that mean you're staying?

                    NICK
          I need some time to think.

Tiffany gets up from her seat.

                    TIFFANY
          I'll wait in the car if...

                    NICK
          No, go ahead and get back to what
          you need to do. This place isn't
          so tough that I can't walk back to
          town alone, even in the dark.

                    TIFFANY
          You have to watch out; these woods
          are full of vicious snipes.

                    NICK
          You still remember that?

                    TIFFANY
          The great snipe hunt of eighty-
          nine? At the first sign of
          Alzheimer's I'm having the tale
          tattooed on my arm so that I can
          relive it every day.

Tiffany glides to the door and turns.

                    TIFFANY
          You know where to find me if you
          need me. Oh, and Nick?

                    NICK
          Yeah?

                    TIFFANY
          Plane enough?!

                    NICK
          That one landed huh? Yeah, I had a
          hard time keeping a straight face.
          It's kind of a terminal condition.
          I get started and I'm like a
          run'way truck.

                    TIFFANY
          Oh, no.

Tiffany flees from Nick's laughter.

INT THE LIMIT - LATER

Nick is packing away bottles of alcohol. VERONICA and JOEY walk in. Nick doesn't look up.

                    NICK
          Bar's closed, come back later.

                    JOEY
          We're not here for drinks.

                    VERONICA
          We just came to see if we still
          had jobs.

Nick looks up.

                    NICK
          Oh, you work here?

                    VERONICA
          Do we?

                    NICK
          For the time being the bar is
          closed. I know that is going to
          put the pinch on you guys. I'll
          have to go through the business
          papers to see if my father had any
          kind of severance package or
          something. With this place being a
          bar and knowing my father, I doubt
          it, but I'll see what I can do.
          Why don't you guys take all this
          alcohol and see what another bar
          will give you for it. Whatever you
          can get for it, it's yours. That's
          about all I can do for you right
          now.

INT BEN'S HOUSE - LATER

Ben is playing an Xbox game. There is a KNOCK at the door. Ben drops the controller letting his character die.

               BEN
     Was gonna restart anyway.

When Ben opens the door he is surprised to see Nick on his porch.

               BEN
     Nick.

               NICK
     Hey. Um, do you mind if I-

               BEN
     Crash with me for a couple of
     days. Sweet. Come on in. Where's
     your stuff?

               NICK
     I left it back in my rental car.
     Couldn't carry much while holding
     on to... Rachelle is it?

               BEN
     You got on her bike with her?

               NICK
     It was either that or walk twenty
     miles.

               BEN
     That is dangerous in more ways
     than one. No worries though. I
     have a spare, unused, toothbrush.

               NICK
     Thanks. Mind if I make a long
     distance call on your phone?

                    BEN
          Just use my cell.

Ben points at his cell phone lying on the table.

                    BEN
          Mi casa es su casa.

Nick dials a number while Ben goes back to his game.

                    NICK
          Emily?... Hi, sorry to call so
          late. The funeral went... well. I
          was hoping that I wouldn't have to
          do this, but I'm going to need a
          couple more days off... The one
          time my father could have made
          things easy for me by ignoring me,
          he ends up willing me his
          business. I don't know how long...
          No, you don't have to do that...
          You're awesome Em. Thanks... I'll
          let you know. Thanks again.

Nick hangs up.

                    BEN
          So, does this mean you're staying
          in town?

                    NICK
          You never know. That's one thing
          that I have learned is you never
          know. What game is that?

                    BEN
          Grab a controller man.

INT BEN'S HOUSE - NEXT MORNING

Ben stumbles out of his bedroom. On the couch are neatly folded blankets and a pillow.

In the kitchen there is a covered plate of pancakes and a note.

NOTE
I used the last of your milk for breakfast. I'll bring some home with me later today. Thanks for letting me crash.

                    BEN
        Shoot, you keep cooking me
        breakfast and you can stay as long
        as you want.

Ben digs into the pancakes.

INT CAFE - MORNING

Nick enters the cafe.

Nick looks around. At one of the tables is a high school student, Jerry, reading The Great Gatsby. He drops the book and scrubs at his face with his hands.

                    JERRY
        Ughh.

Nick gets up and takes a seat next to him.

                    NICK
        What's the problem?

                    JERRY
        This story is so boring.

                    NICK
        What chapter are you on?

                    JERRY
        Two. I can't stand it. Nothing is
        happening. It's just a whole bunch
        of blah.

                    NICK
          Trust me it doesn't really get any
          better.

                    JERRY
          And I have to write an essay on
          this.

                    NICK
          Here's what helped me in school.

INT CAFE BACKROOM - LATER

Rachelle is sitting in the back eating breakfast.
Nick pokes his head around the corner.

                    NICK
          You need to get out more.

                    RACHELLE
          It's my day off. I'm just here for
          the food.

                    NICK
          Is Tiffany around?

                    RACHELLE
          Not yet. If she were she would
          probably try and con me into
          working her shift. What's up?

                    NICK
          I need a ride to the hospital and
          was hoping that-

                    RACHELLE
          I'll take you.

                    NICK
          Serious?

                    RACHELLE
          It will give me a good excuse to
          not pick up the extra shift. Have
          you eaten?

                    NICK
          Yeah.

                    RACHELLE
          Then let's clear out before
          Tyrannosaurus-Tiff shows up.

EXT HOSPITAL

Nick stops at a little flower vendor's place and buys two lilies.

INT ELEVATOR

The doors close and Nick steps back from the control panel.

                    RACHELLE
          Okay, I gotta ask. Why two lilies?

                    NICK
          They're for my mother. She loved
          the smell of lilies.

                    RACHELLE
          But two? It's kind of an odd, even
          number. Seems like there's a
          little more there.

                    NICK
          One for me and one for my sister.

The elevator doors open and they exit.

INT HOSPITAL HALL

Nick and Rachelle continue their conversation as they pass through the hall.

                    RACHELLE
          I didn't know you had a sister?
          Tiffany never mentioned more
          family than your mother and
          father.

                    NICK
          I had a younger sister. We used to
          pick or buy, or steal lilies for
          my mother. So, one from each of
          us.

Nick stops at a door. He takes a slow, deep breath
and goes in.

INT NICK'S MOM'S HOSPITAL ROOM

Monitors beep, respirators hiss, and tubes snake
all over a woman's body. Rachelle stifles an "oh".

Nick untucks one of his mother's arms from her
sheets and places the lilies in her fingers. She
doesn't flinch or register that anything is going
on.

                    NICK
          Hi mom, it's Nick.

Rachelle slides quietly into the hall.

                    NICK
          I know that it's been a while.
          It's been more than a while. I
          couldn't ... didn't want to come
          back. My father died. He willed me
          The Limit. What am I going to do
          with a bar? I thought about
          selling it. That way I could pay
          the hospital a little longer, in
          case... in case you decide to get
          up. But, you aren't getting up,
          are you?

Nick gets up and looks out the window. Outside the
landscape is classic, beautiful Midwest.

                    NICK
          It's so different from the city.
          God I wish I knew what the last
          letter you were able to read was.
          I kept sending them. Where do I
          start?

INT HOSPITAL HALLWAY - LATER

Rachelle sits in a chair reading a magazine. Nick
exits the room quietly. He steps up in front of
Rachelle.

                    NICK
          Sorry I took so long. Ready to go?

                    RACHELLE
          Are you sure? You can stay longer.
          This is a fascinating article.

                    NICK
          Hey, you waited for me, I can wait
          for you to finish reading an
          article.

Rachelle sets the article aside and jumps up.

                    RACHELLE
          Well, I was lying about the
          article. I just didn't want you to
          feel bad. I don't want to rush
          you.

Nick cocks his head catching a hint of another
meaning.

                    RACHELLE
          Into leaving, I mean, if you
          needed more time or had anything
          else you had to do. I'm free all
          day. This is getting me my good-
          karma-brownie-points.

                    NICK
          You need a lot of those?

                    RACHELLE
          Depends on who you ask.

                    NICK
          Well, if anybody asks me you
          deserve a ton. Thanks.

EXT HOSPITAL

Nick and Rachelle are walking toward her
motorcycle.

                    RACHELLE
          Do you mind if I ask what happened
          to your mom?

                    NICK
          It's complicated. There was an
          accident. She wasn't like this at
          first. Over the years things went
          downhill.

                    RACHELLE
          Oh no.

                    NICK
          What?

Nick looks up. There is a beat-up pick-up parked
on the street behind Rachelle's motorcycle. TODD
is leaning against the hood.

                    RACHELLE
          It's Todd.

                    NICK
          Boyfriend?

                    RACHELLE
          Ex. I don't think he understands
          that ex is only a variable in
          algebra. Of course, I'm not sure
          he ever took algebra.

                    TODD
          Hey Rachelle.

                    RACHELLE
          Todd.

                    TODD
          Who's this?

                    RACHELLE
          This is Nick.

                    TODD
          You must be Riley's kid.

Todd puts his hand out. Nick shakes it. Todd gives
it an extra squeeze as he lets go. He puts his arm
around Rachelle.

                    TODD
          I ended up with two tickets for
          that band you like, Bloody Rocks
          or something.

                    RACHELLE
          Blood From A Stone.

                    TODD
          Yeah, them. This Friday, we can
          have dinner and...

                    NICK
          I'll leave you guys alone.

                    RACHELLE
          No you don't have to.

Rachelle brushes his arm off.

                    RACHELLE
          I'm busy Friday.

                    TODD
          With what?

                    RACHELLE
          With not going out with you. How
          many times are we going to do
          this?

                    TODD
          Do what?

                    RACHELLE
          We broke up. It's over.

                    TODD
          Since when?

                    RACHELLE
          Since you decided that Nikki
          needed mouth to mouth at the
          drive-in. What did you think I
          meant when I said, "we're done,"
          and stormed off?

                    TODD
          That was three months ago.

                    RACHELLE
          And it still applies today, and
          tomorrow, and the day after.

                    TODD
          So you'd rather hang out with this
          dweeb than me?

                    RACHELLE
          Hey, leave him out of this.

Nick breaks out laughing.

                    NICK
          I can't believe you used the word
          dweeb with a straight face.

                    TODD
          You think this is funny?

                    NICK
          I think that it doesn't matter
          what I say, you're going to be
          angry either way, so I might as
          well find some humor in it. What
          matters is what you are going to
          do with your anger. You can thrash
          me right in front of a hospital,
          which isn't going to score you any
          points with her, or you can leave
          me out of your argument.

Todd looks stunned for a moment. He turns and stomps to his truck and drives off.

                    RACHELLE
          What was that?

                    NICK
          What?

                    RACHELLE
          What you did to get rid of Todd?
          How did you do that?

                    NICK
          I just took things to the most
          extreme end they could have gone
          and let it appeal to his rational
          side.

                    RACHELLE
          I didn't know he had a rational
          side.

                    NICK
          Everybody does, you just have to
          dig a bit deeper in some than
          others.

                    RACHELLE
          Just be careful. Todd has a brutal
          bark and a bite that's just as
          bad.

INT CAFE - LATER

Rachelle is behind the bar now. Nick and Tiffany
are talking over mugs of coffee.

                    NICK
          One of the hardest things is
          wondering how someone can look so
          completely healthy and yet not be
          there.

                    TIFFANY
          What did the doctor have to say?

                    NICK
          I didn't talk to the doctor. I did
          two weeks ago and it was the same
          as a month before, and a month
          before that. I've decided that...
          I'll give people a couple of days
          to say their goodbyes and then...
          well, then I kill my mother.

                    TIFFANY
          Don't think about it like that.
          You aren't killing your mother.
          You aren't betraying her or
          letting her down. You're letting
          her go.

                    NICK
          But I'll always be asking myself
          "what if?" What if one more day
          was all she needed? What if some
          doctor comes out with a new
          technique?

                    TIFFANY
          And what if she never ever gets
          better? What if from day one there
          was never any chance for her? What
          if being on life support is
          torture for her but she has no way
          to let you know? You may never
          know the answers to any of these
          questions Nick, but that doesn't
          matter. You aren't doing this to
          get rid of a burden, you aren't
          giving up on someone, you aren't
          thinking about yourself and that
          is what matters. You are thinking
          about her, your heart is in the
          right place.

INT THE LIMIT - LATER

An envelope lies on the ground as if it has been
pushed under the door. The door opens and Nick
steps on the envelope as he walks in.

                    NICK
          What's this?

Nick picks up the envelope and opens it. There are
a few, hundred dollar bills and a note.

Nick reads the note out loud.

                    NICK
          Mr. Grant, your father and I had
          an arrangement. Here is your cut
          of last month's business. I hope
          this clears up any mishaps that
          may have occurred and will prevent
          any further...What the?

Nick crumples up the note and stares at the money.

INT THE LIMIT OFFICE - EVENING

There are stacks of paperwork everywhere. The note and the hundreds rest on a shelf above the desk. Nick is flipping through a file.

Nick comes across a fire permit for the Limit. He sets that aside and continues going through the paperwork.

Outside TIRES SCRUNCH to a stop behind the building.

                    NICK
    Oh no you don't.

INT THE LIMIT BAR

Nick exits the office. He grabs a pool cue as he passes through the room and heads for the rear.

EXT THE LIMIT

A car has pulled to a stop behind the bar. The car's door opens and as the driver steps out Nick bursts out of the bar with the cue raised.

                    NICK
    Get out of here you-

The driver yells and raises his hands and his face is revealed, the Pastor.

                    PASTOR
    Nicholas!

                    NICK
    Whoa.

Nick lowers the cue stick.

NICK
Sorry about that, I thought you were someone else.

PASTOR
Who?

NICK
Someone who was using my property as a place to sell drugs. He thinks that he can pay me off.

PASTOR
I commend your desire, but you can't come charging out and starting a fight. What if he had a gun?

NICK
I didn't think, I just reacted.

PASTOR
Our security is not a matter of weapons alone. The arm that wields them must be strong, the eye that guides them must be clear, and the will that directs them indomitable.

NICK
Bible verse?

PASTOR
Franklin D. Roosevelt.

NICK
Hm. So what brings you out to the Limit, Pastor?

PASTOR
I wanted to talk to you Nick.
(MORE)

PASTOR (CONT'D)
The town is buzzing with talk first about the funeral, closing the bar, and now your mother.

NICK
People are upset huh?

PASTOR
Quite a few.

NICK
So they send the Pastor out to talk to the prodigal son.

PASTOR
I wouldn't say that you are a prodigal son. See, the people here aren't used to change like this. Your father and his place were very well known and liked. They hate to see his memory blackened like this.

NICK
Really? Did they know that my father was letting the local drug dealer do his business on his property? Did they know that he was taking a cut from that drug money? They want to remember him as a good person, but he wasn't.

PASTOR
All have sinned and fallen short of the kingdom of God. They don't judge him.

NICK
But they'll judge me for taking my mother off life support? Come on.

                    PASTOR
          I wouldn't say that they are
          judging you.

                    NICK
          But they're upset by my decision?
          No, I don't think this has
          anything to do with my mother.
          That's the problem, nothing ever
          did. She was a city girl. My
          father brought her to Littletown
          USA, but she was always seen as
          the girl from the city. This is
          about my father and his bar.
          Here's the thing. I own this bar
          and this land. It is mine to do
          with as I see fit. I have had to
          live with the consequences of my
          father's actions and no one saw
          fit to correct him. Where were
          they when I was hungry at home?
          Where were they when I was
          struggling to put myself through
          school? They were laughing it up
          with my father. So those same
          people can just keep their
          opinions to themselves. If you'll
          excuse me, Pastor, I have some
          more work to do.

INT THE LIMIT

Nick shuts the door and walks to the middle of the
room. Outside the Pastor's CAR DRIVES OFF.

Nick throws the pool cue across the room. There is
a KNOCK at the front door. Nick opens the door.
Jerry is there with a girl.

                    JERRY
          Uh, I asked around and heard you
          were here.

                    NICK
          Oh it's you... sorry, forgot your
          name?

                    JERRY
          Jerry. This is my girlfriend,
          Courtney.

                    NICK
          Nice to meet you. What are you
          guys doing out here?

                    JERRY
          Well, those things you told me
          really helped. We have to write
          this essay on the first parts of
          the book and I was kind of hoping
          that you could help us out with
          that. Unless you have things to do
          I know that-

                    NICK
          Actually, I don't really. Come in.

                    COURTNEY
          Are we allowed to? Isn't this a
          bar?

                    NICK
          Not any more. Why don't you guys
          grab a table?

INT THE LIMIT - LATER

Jerry and Courtney are working on their essays.
Nick enters the room from the kitchen with a
massive plate of nachos.

                    NICK
          Break time. You guys have been at
          this for three hours. You need
          something to keep your brains
          going.

Nick sets the plate down and the two teens dig in. Nick sits at the table and starts writing on a piece of paper.

                    JERRY
          What are you working on?

                    NICK
          A letter to the editor.

                    COURTNEY
          About?

                    NICK
          Local dubiously self-employed
          entrepreneurs.

                    JERRY
          Not sure what that means, but
          okay. Before I forget, I just want
          to say thanks for helping us out
          like this.

                    COURTNEY
          Me too. I know that you are going
          through a rough time right now,
          with your dad passing and all.

                    NICK
          Helping you guys out has been... I
          don't know, kind of therapeutic.
          Besides, I remember when I was
          your age in school. It seemed like
          nobody cared about what we were
          learning, not our teachers and not
          us. We just wanted to get through
          the work. You guys seem like you
          really want to learn.

                    COURTNEY
          We do. I want to go to medical
          school.
                    (MORE)

COURTNEY (CONT'D)
It's just that Literature has nothing to do with healing people and I struggle with it, but if I don't get a good grade, then schools are going to overlook me.

NICK
(To Jerry)
What about you?

JERRY
Not sure yet what I want to do. Probably nothing that has to do with plotlines and metaphors. Instruction manuals are easy reading.

NICK
I'm glad that I could help you out. Let me read what you guys have so far.

INT MOUNT AYR PRESS - NEXT MORNING

Nick enters the door. The secretary looks up.

SECRETARY
Can I help you?

NICK
I have a letter for the editor here. I would type it up, but I don't have a computer. I'm just back for my father's funeral.

SECRETARY
You must be Nick Grant. We've gotten quite a few letters concerning you in the last few days. Do you always stir up a place like this?

                    NICK
          You know, I don't think I managed
          to stir up as much as a ripple in
          California.

                    SECRETARY
          You're really making waves here.

                    NICK
          Well then this letter should fit
          right in.

He hands the letter to the secretary. She scans
it, her eyes widening.

                    NICK
          Do you think that will get
          published? I'll find a way to type
          it up if it needs to be typed.

                    SECRETARY
          I'll go ahead and do that. I need
          something to do. I've already
          painted my nails. Is there
          anything else that I can do for
          you?

Nick shakes his head and leaves. The secretary
sets the paper next to her monitor and starts
typing reading half aloud.

                    SECRETARY
          To the smack-peddling slime ball
          who thinks he can use my property
          to sell drugs...

INT CAFE - DAY

Nick is waiting at the register. Tiffany exits the
back.

                    TIFFANY
          Hey nick, what's up?

                    NICK
          I was wondering if you wanted to
          give me a hand going through some
          of the stuff left at the bar.

                    TIFFANY
          Sure, it'll be like shopping
          without spending the money.

INT THE LIMIT - LATER

Nick holds up an elk head. Tiffany gives it a
thumbs down.

Tiffany points at the jukebox. Nick shakes his
head and gives it a thumbs up.

Nick is up on a ladder taking down the smoke
detector. There is no battery in it.

A large rat pokes its head out of a hole in the
wall. Tiffany jumps away.

Tiffany snags some ice from the ice maker and
stuffs it down Nick's back.

Nick grabs the fountain drink gun at the bar and
shoots Tiffany with a stream of soda water.

EXT THE LIMIT

Nick and Tiffany sit on the roof watching the sun
light flicker through the tops of the trees.

                    NICK
          Thanks for all the help.

                    TIFFANY
          It was fun, except for that beast
          that lives in there.

                    NICK
          That's definitely a legendary rat.

Nick's watch goes off. He turns the alarm off.

                    TIFFANY
          What's that for?

                    NICK
          It's time.

                    TIFFANY
          Tonight?

INT HOSPITAL HALL - LATER

The elevator door opens and Nick steps out with a dozen lilies. Tiffany follows. The hall is tinged orange by the sunset glow slipping through the windows.

INT HOSPITAL ROOM

Nick and Tiffany stand next to the bed while a doctor is explaining things to them. A nurse stands by with a clipboard.

                    DOC
          Once the breathing machine is
          removed your mother will probably
          take a few shallow breaths on her
          own and then expire. Would you
          like some time alone?

                    NICK
          I've said everything I need to
          say. You?

Nick looks at Tiffany. She nods her head.

Nick kisses his mother on the forehead. He removes her breathing apparatus and holds the lilies so that her last breaths will catch the scent of the bouquet. She takes a few shallow breaths and then dies. Her monitor flat lines and the nurse shuts it off after the slightest beep.

Nick folds his mother's hands over the bouquet on her chest. As Nick steps back Tiffany takes his hand in hers. They leave while the nurse records the time of death.

EXT HOSPITAL - NIGHT

Nick and Tiffany exit. Nick stops.

                    NICK
          I think that I'm going to walk
          back.

                    TIFFANY
          Are you sure?

                    NICK
          Yeah, I could use the fresh air.

                    TIFFANY
          Okay, just be careful.

                    NICK
          Tiff...

                    TIFFANY
          Yeah.

                    NICK
          Thanks, for everything.

Tiffany watches Nick walk off into the night.

EXT MOUNT AYR - NIGHT

There are no streetlights along the rural road. Nick stays off by the trees for the most part. The moonlight illuminates the road.

Nick is speared by headlights and then the car is passed. The car breaks and pulls off to the side. When Nick gets closer the driver's side door pops open and the Drug Dealer gets out with a stick in hand.

                      DRUG DEALER
         Who do you think you are?

                      NICK
         What?

                      DRUG DEALER
         You think that article was funny?

                      NICK
         I wasn't trying to be funny at
         all. Look, I don't want any
         trouble-

                      DRUG DEALER
         Then you should have taken the
         money and kept your mouth shut.

                      NICK
         Or maybe you shouldn't be selling
         drugs. Why don't you try becoming
         a productive member of society
         instead of tearing people down?
         You are a failure as a human
         being.

The drug Dealer lunges at Nick with a wild swing. He barely misses and Nick closes the distance making the stick mostly useless. They struggle for a while and the stick goes flying.

The Drug Dealer gains the upper hand. He shoves Nick's face to the ground and manages to jump up and repeatedly kick Nick in the ribs. Nick curls into a ball trying to protect himself.

Headlights flare as a car rounds the bend. The Drug Dealer delivers one more kick and bolts to his car. As the new arrival pulls off the road next to Nick the Drug Dealer peels out and speeds off.

Nick tries to get up. The driver of the new car hops out.

                    DRIVER
          Hey you... are you all right?

Nick collapses back down with a groan and rolls onto his back.

                    DRIVER
          I'm calling nine-one-one.

INT CAFÉ - NEXT DAY

Tiffany is ringing up a customer. Nick enters quite beat up.

                    TIFFANY
          Geez Nick, what happened to you?

                    NICK
          My letter to the editor was not
          well received.

                    TIFFANY
          You look like you should be in
          bed.

                    NICK
          Maybe, but I wanted you to be the
          first to know that I've decided to
          stay.

Tiffany gestures to his injuries. A line of customers is starting to form behind Nick.

                    TIFFANY
          After that?

                    NICK
          Because of, maybe, I don't know.
                    (MORE)

                    NICK (CONT'D)
          I'm going to stay. I'm going to
          turn The Limit into a place that
          helps people, not drags them down.

                    TIFFANY
          Okay, but what?

                    NICK
          I'm not sure yet. All I know is
          that I have a bunch more work to
          do.

                    CUSTOMER
          Come on, either buy something or
          move on.

                    TIFFANY
          I'd better take care of them.

Nick heads for the door. He turns with a wicked smile.

                    NICK
          Hey, Tiffany.

Tiffany and the whole line look.

                    TIFFANY
          Yeah.

                    NICK
          Maybe I'll start an etiquette
          school.

The woman gives Nick a withering look.

INT THE LIMIT - LATER

Nick is failing miserably to get the juke box to work.

There is a knock at the door. Nick abandons the project and answers the door.

Tiffany is there with LYNN ROSS.

>   TIFFANY
> Lynn came by the café. She wants
> to interview you about, well,
> everything.

>   LYNN
> If you don't mind Mr. Grant?
> You've got the town all stirred
> up. I know this is really soon
> after your mother and..., I can
> come back another time if you
> want.

>   NICK
> Now is fine, but I really don't
> know what to tell you.

EXT THE LIMIT

Nick steps out into the sun light. Tiffany and Lynn follow.

>   LYNN
> You could start with how you got
> those cuts and bruises.

>   NICK
> I had a run in with a disgruntled
> business associate of my father's.

>   LYNN
> They were upset about you closing
> the bar?

>   NICK
> He was upset that I wouldn't let
> him sell drugs on my property.

> LYNN
> So that letter to the editor you wrote...

> NICK
> Was exactly what happened? I received a note and a bribe from someone. Last night I was walking back from the hospital and we had an altercation. We had differing opinions about my article.

> LYNN
> So, Tiffany tells me that you have decided to stay in Mount Ayr. You've closed your father's business. What are you planning to do?

> NICK
> I don't know. I want to do something worth doing, but I haven't figured out what.

A car pulls into the parking lot. Nick, Tiffany, and Lynn watch as Jerry gets out of the car. His mother, STACY, gets out of the front with a pie in her hands.

> JERRY
> There he is.

Stacy walks up and hands the pie to Nick. She then hugs him and kisses him on the cheek.

> STACY
> Thank you so much. I'm Jerry's mom. Jerry got an A on his paper. He told me that you helped him with writing it and well thank you. He's never been this happy in school.
> (More)

                    STACY (CONT'D)
          I, well, I love him no matter what
          grades he gets but... neither of
          us can stop smiling today.

                    JERRY
          Uh, I have another paper and I was
          hoping you could...

                    NICK
          Help you on it. Sure.

                    JERRY
          I'll get my stuff from the car.

Stacy hugs Nick one more time and then leaves.
Jerry pulls his stuff out of the car and his
mother hands him something.

Jerry returns.

                    JERRY
          My mom told me to give you this
          when she was gone so it would be
          too late for you to return it.

Jerry hands Nick a check.

                    JERRY
          Would you be upset if I told some
          of my friends about getting help
          here? I know a couple other guys
          that could use some help. They'd
          pay.

                    NICK
          Let's see if I can help you get
          another A first, just to make sure
          it wasn't a fluke.

                    JERRY
          Cool.

Jerry heads into The Limit.

Lynn is scribbling on her note pad as fast as she can.

                   TIFFANY
     So, still unsure what you're going
     to do?

                   NICK
     I think I'm getting an idea.

                   TIFFANY
     Looks like you've got a good
     start.

                   NICK
     With pie. Maybe that's what The
     Limit will be, a help center slash
     restaurant.

EXT CEMETARY - TWO DAYS LATER

Nick, Tiffany, and several others are watching Nick's mother's casket being lowered into the ground right next to the fresh grave of Nick's father. The Pastor is noticeably absent.

                   NICK
     This was one of my mother's
     favorite poems.

     Hurry, hurry the day has come,
     There's not enough time
     To do what need be done.

     Break your fast
     Dress your bones
     Step, step quick
     To day's unknowns.
                   (MORE)

                    NICK (CONT'D)
          Hurry, hurry it's noon so fast,
          There's such finite time
          In which the day is cast.

          Catch the bus
          Pick up clothes
          Step, step quick
          To noon's disclose.

          Hurry, hurry the eve is drawn
          There's dwindling time
          Where has day now gone?

          Take a bath
          Say a prayer
          Step step quick
          To midnight's cares.

          Delay, delay your life has past,
          Such squandered time
          Once gone can not be grasped.

          Take your time
          Love as God
          Step, step slow
          To death's repose.

The casket is covered and the crowd disperses.

EXT HILLTOP TREE - EVENING

Nick and Tiffany are sitting in the branches.

                    TIFFANY
          I never thought that I'd be back
          up here.

                    NICK
          How come?

                    TIFFANY
          I was getting too old, too grown
          up. The friend who taught me to
          climb was gone.

169

They share a quiet moment.

                       TIFFANY
        What made you decide to bury your mother next to your father?

                       NICK
        I loved my mother so much. So often when I was a child she was my strength. She so loved my father. I... I hated my father. She always wanted me to love him. How could I hate someone that she so loved? If I visit my mother then I have to visit my father. I may not love him, but I don't, not want to. We all have our limits and when we are there we need someone to help get us through. My mother was always that person, this way, she still is.

They settle back against the tree and watch the sun set.

                                                      END

This is a rough draft that I literally just finished this week. It is really the first, original, full length play that I have ever written. A few years ago a friend had me write what was basically a collection of skits that fell in order. It was "The Bible in Shorts", which was a take off on "The Complete Works of William Shakespeare Abridged." As of yet I got through the Old Testament, and it has sat since then.

The idea for this play hit me while I was writing down the idea for another play during the intermission of the play that I was seeing.

A Dollar Short

Jake	A writer who has just gotten his big break with an esteemed publishing company.
Molly	Jake's beautiful, across-the-hall neighbor who takes care of her father.
Garford Jenkins	The owner of the Tabularasa publishing company.
Cilia	Garford's young assistant.
Haberdash	An old-timer who is friends with Jake. He means well, but is usually a bit slow on the uptake.
Milton	The obnoxious, "slimy", scumbag owner of Jake and Molly's apartment complex.
Phoney	A slacking electronics delivery and installation man.
Phoney 2	Phoney's partner in laziness.
Beggar	A good-natured yet practical homeless man.

Waitress	The waitress who works at the coffee shop.
Connie	A well-to-do pregnant woman who finds herself in a rough spot.
Con	A streetwise three card monte hustler.
Shill	One of Con's cronies. Would cheat his own mother if he could.
Frank	A city works employee working on the bridge early in the morning.
Knitting Woman	An absentminded lady knitting in the cafe.

Setting

The setting is generic New York. The Tabularasa Publishing offices and the Ratherby apartments, as well as the city streets and a rooftop.

Time

The entirety of the play takes place from Friday evening to Saturday morning.

Act I

Scene 1

(The Tabularasa Publishing Company. Garford Jenkins is in his office and Cilia is at her desk. Jake enters the scene completely dejected and disheveled, Cilia knocks on the office door, and everyone freezes. Jake steps out of character.)

(As Jake talks about his day he straightens himself up, puts on a tie, shines shoes, combs his hair, etc.)

JAKE
I don't even know why I'm back here. I blew it. My one chance, my big break and I blew it. It started out last night with a meeting in this same office with Garford Jenkins, the head of one of the most respected publishing houses in New York. People say that if they decided to publish your to-do list it would be a best seller just because of their reputation. After four years I had finally gotten an opportunity to pitch to Mr. Jenkins and I had a winner. Four years of work destroyed.

(Jake steps back into character. The lights move so that it seems like the sun goes down and comes back up to a sunset, the large clock runs backwards, Jake, Garford and Cilia go about things backwards.)

(Jake enters the office backwards, sits down, takes his notebook off the desk, and pantomimes talking. Time becomes normal.)

JAKE
... And the Rose of Morning sails off into a sunset much like this one.

>   (Jake sets his notebook on the
>   desk.)

                        GARFORD
So ends the story.

                         JAKE
That's it.

                        GARFORD
Son, that was the most marvelous waste of time
I've had in three weeks. And that's saying
something considering I've been to two political
rallies and spent a week with my mother-in-law.
Tell you what; I'm going to give you a second
shot. I have an important meeting here tomorrow so
here's what's going to happen, you are going to
come back here tomorrow morning and present
another idea to me.

                         JAKE
Tomorrow morning.

                        GARFORD
Tomorrow morning, at eight sharp. Cilia will
validate your parking for you. Good evening.

>   (Jake is led out by Cilia.)

                         JAKE
I don't believe this.

                         CILIA
Can I see your parking permit?

                         JAKE
I... I took a cab.

                         CILIA
Well then, we'll see you bright and early tomorrow
morning. Good evening.

>   (Jake enters one of the elevators.
>   Mr. G packs up his things. Cilia

picks up the notebook with several other papers.)

GARFORD

Cilia, how about we check out a bit early. I wanted to take the misses to a play tonight and unless my memory is failing I believe you have been spending some extra time with a certain young man who delivers the mail.

CILIA

Thank you Mr. G.

(They enter the other elevator.)

JAKE

A brand new idea over night. And better than the one I've been working years on. That's not possible. There were nine months of research alone I had done to get everything just right. Well, maybe it didn't have to be brand new.

(Exits Elevator)

JAKE

After all I was constantly putting things in my notebook... my notebook, which I had left sitting on Mr. G's desk. Oh man!

(Dashes back into the elevator.)

CILIA

May I be candid sir?

GARFORD

Always.

CILIA

I thought you were a bit harsh on that young man.

GARFORD

Had to be.

(Garford and Cilia exit.)

(Jake dashes out of the elevator.)

JAKE

Mrs. Cilia, Mr. Jenkins, I... Where is everybody? You can't be gone. I was just here and... I need my notebook.

(Peers through Garford's window)

JAKE

No, no, no.

(He hangs his head and makes his way back to the elevator. End of scene one)

Act I

Scene 2

(Jake takes to the streets. There is a woman knitting at an outdoor cafe.)

JAKE
You can do this. All you need is an idea. It just has to be something that's new. But what's new. There are only so many plots. It took me forever to
        (pause)
No, don't think about the past. You are here and now and this is what you have to work with.

(Haberdash enters.)

HABERDASH
Jake, Jake Sulivan, is that you?

JAKE
It's me Mr. Haberdash.

HABERDASH
What are you doing out alone on a Friday night my boy?

JAKE
I'm trying to come up with an idea.

HABERDASH
What kind of idea?

JAKE
Any idea. I have to present it to Garford Jenkins tomorrow morning.

HABERDASH
Garford Jenkins. You mean the publisher?

JAKE
Yeah.

                    HABERDASH
You mean you finally got a meeting with him?

                        JAKE
I did.

                    HABERDASH
And you didn't have an idea for a book. Kids these days.

                        JAKE
I had an idea.

                    HABERDASH
What happened to it?

                        JAKE
He... he didn't like it. He gave me tonight to come up with a new idea, and I can't think of anything.

                    HABERDASH
Sounds like you're in for a long night.

                        JAKE
I should probably get to work.

                (Jake tries to leave)

                    HABERDASH
You know, this reminds me of a time back when I was about your age.

                (Jake stops to listen)

                    HABERDASH
Me and Ramsey, not Erickson, but the other one. The one that used to live on the other side of little falls back before there was the... or was it after the Hackensack... no it was before. He lived out there and he and I used to run over to Mr. Dunne's garage. Mr. Dunne had this great big old Great Dane, had a spot right on his back. Everyone called 'im target except for Mr. Dunne. In fact, I was thinking about him just the other day. One of those old Ford's park outside, looked

exactly like one of the ones that Dunne used to fix for folks.

JAKE

Mr. Haberdash? Mr. Haberdash. I don't want to be rude but I really have to get to work.

HABERDASH

No time like the present.

>(Mr. Haberdash exits. Jake yawns.)

JAKE

No way. I can't get tired now.

>(Sees the coffee shop.)

JAKE

I'll just get some coffee.

>(Jake takes a seat at the outdoor cafe. A waitress comes to his table.)

WAITRESS

What can I get you?

JAKE

A coffee with an extra shot of espresso. You know what, better make it two extra shots.

WAITRESS

Two extra shots. Sounds like you have a long night ahead of you. You want to pay now?

JAKE

Sure.

>(He hands her a five dollar bill. She leaves and two women stop to look at the cafe snacks. Jake is piqued by their conversation and moves closer.)

LADY 1

And he carries her off. The police and army are after them. It's just like when they first met except it's here not there, but he still sees himself as king so

>   (She notices Jake listening in.)

LADY 1

Can I help you?

JAKE

You may have. I'm sorry, I overheard a bit of what you were saying and it sounds like a perfect story. Which king were you talking about?

LADY 1

Movie in fact. King Kong.

>   (Jake hangs his head and returns
>   to slump in his seat. The ladies
>   exit.)

LADY 2

Wonder what that was all about?

LADY 1

I haven't the slightest idea. Anyway...

>   (Waitress returns)

WAITRESS

Here you go. Three fifty out of five, your change is one fifty. Course, you might want to switch to tea. You look really stressed.

>   (Sets change on his table.)

JAKE

I am really stressed. Have you ever had one of those days that were supposed to be perfect and instead you find the rug pulled out from under you and it's a long drop?

WAITRESS

Nope. Of course, I've never expected a day to be perfect. All days are opportunities, some to shine, some to enjoy, and others to make us stronger.

JAKE

That's it.

WAITRESS

What's it?

JAKE

Pen, I need a pen. Find me a pen.

(They scurry to find a pen.)

JAKE

Ma'am, do you have a pen I could borrow?

(The knitting woman sets aside her work and grabs her purse.)

KNITTING WOMAN

Let's see. Mascara, you wouldn't want that, lipstick, breath mints. Would you like a mint?

JAKE

No, thank you. I just really need that pen.

KNITTING WOMAN

Hair brush, hair ties, hair gel, well I have a veritable salon in here don't I?

(Jake abandons the woman. Waitress comes out with a pen.)

JAKE

Ah ha.

(Takes the pen.)

JAKE

Paper.

(Spots the dollar bills on the table. Grabs them and writes on one.)

WAITRESS
Hey, what are you doing?

JAKE
Shhh, hold on.

WAITRESS
You know that's a federal offense.

JAKE
Yes, yes, this is going to be perfect.

(Finishes writing)

JAKE
It may be a federal offense, but trust me, this idea is worth it. Now, time to get to work.

(Kisses the dollar and exits. Knitting woman looks up from her purse.)

KNITTING WOMAN
Nope no pen, sorry, I... hello?

(End of scene two.)

Act I

Scene 3

(The Ratherby Apartment Complex. The Landlord is in the hall arguing with Molly.)

MOLLY
My hours were cut this week, it's all I have.

MILTON
Well it's not enough.

(Jake enters)

MOLLY
You can't just kick us out like this.

MILTON
I can and will. You have till tomorrow morning to get your stuff out of the apartment.

MOLLY
Where are we going to go? My father is sick and-

JAKE
What's going on?

MOLLY
I'm short on rent and he's kicking me and my father out.

JAKE
Okay, you can stay with me.

MILTON
Better not. That would violate your rental agreement. You'll be on the streets too.

JAKE
Well, how much are you short.

MOLLY
Thirty six dollars.

> (Jake pulls out his wallet)

JAKE
I have thirty five dollars. Will that do?

MILTON
Still a dollar short.

JAKE
You have got to be kidding.

MOLLY
It's just one dollar.

MILTON
It's my building.

> (Jake gets into his pocket.)

JAKE
And fifty cents. How's that? The banks are closed and I don't have an ATM card, so can you wait on fifty cents. You can charge interest.

MILTON
Still short.

MOLLY
Please.

> (Jake looks at his idea dollar.)

JAKE
Here, that's thirty six dollars.

> (Milton glowers at Jake, and then snatches the money. Molly leaps to hug Jake.)

MOLLY
Oh thankyouthankyouthankyou.

> (Milton begins stomping off.)

JAKE
Wait.

(Disengages from Molly.)

JAKE

I need to see that dollar. I wrote an idea on it and I can't-

MILTON

Too bad, it's mine now. If you want to buy it back be my guest.

JAKE

How much?

MILTON

Three dollars.

JAKE

Three dollars that's-

MILTON

What the price is. Do you want your idea or not?

(Milton exits.)

MOLLY

He's so rotten. If he wants us out so badly why not just kick us out.

JAKE

He can't. He has to find some violation to kick you out. As long as you meet the requirements of your rental agreement to the letter he can't do anything that you couldn't sue for.

MOLLY

Well I'm sorry about your dollar. Can I help you get the three dollars?

JAKE

Thanks. Check your cushions, and the ones in my place. I'll hit the street.

MOLLY

Got it.

(They exit. End of scene three)

Act I

Scene 4

(Jake takes to the streets asking passers-by for money. He catches the eye of a beggar.)

JAKE

Change ma'am. All I need is some change. Sir, could you spare a quarter. It's an emergency.

BEGGAR

Never gonna work like that son. They've heard the "it's an emergency line" day in and out.

JAKE

But it really is an emergency, not a medical one, but it is.

BEGGAR

Maybe it is, maybe it ain't. Still, you ain't gonna get any pity out of them. 'Specially dressed like that. You don't look homeless.

JAKE

But I'm not.

BEGGAR

What are you out pan handling for then? You aren't one of them lazy 'Mericans that just don't want to work?

JAKE

No, I have a job. I just need three dollars to buy back my dollar.

BEGGAR

Three for one, sounds like a lousy trade to me.

JAKE

Yeah, but I wrote something down on the dollar and the idea was worth more than three dollars.

BEGGAR

What was the idea?

                    JAKE
I can't remember. I got sidetracked.

                    BEGGAR
Beautiful woman?

                    JAKE
Something like that. Any way, I had to use the dollar to pay her rent and now I need to buy it back.

                    BEGGAR
Well shoot, I've got three dollars.

                    JAKE
Would you lend them to me? I'll pay you back.

                    BEGGAR
With interest?

                    JAKE
Five dollars, tomorrow morning.

                    BEGGAR
Deal.

            (They shake and the beggar gives
            Jake the money. End of scene four)

Act I

Scene 5

(The Ratherby apartments. Jake runs down the hall and pounds on Milton's door. Molly enters the hall from Jake's apartment. Milton answers his door.)

MOLLY

Did you get it?

JAKE

I got it.

MILTON

That is three dollars.

JAKE

Now, where's my dollar?

MILTON

Gone.

JAKE & MOLLY

What?!

MILTON

They just delivered my new T.V. They moved it in for me and everything. I couldn't just not tip them.

JAKE

No. You son of a-

MOLLY

Who were they?

MILTON

Two young men. Said I was their last stop and then they were off to get a few drinks. Some place called the...

JAKE

The what?

MILTON
What's it worth to you?

JAKE
All I have is three dollars, and you know that.

(Milton holds out his hand.)

MOLLY
You are horrible.

(Jake pays him.)

MILTON
Place called the 675 Bar.

(Jake exits at a run.)

MOLLY
You're scum, you know that?

(Milton shrugs and shuts the door in her face.)

MOLLY
Jake! Wait for me.

(Exits at a run. Blackout. End Scene Five.)

Act II

Scene 1

(Outside the 675 Bar. Jake and Molly enter.)

MOLLY
There it is. How are we going to find these guys?

JAKE
You didn't see them earlier?

MOLLY
I was too busy looking for change. By the way, your couch cushions are really clean.

(Two guys exit the 675, obviously drunk. One is on the phone.)

PHONEY
Sure thing. We were just about to make the last delivery now.

(Hangs up)

PHONEY 2
I thought you said the truck was clear.

PHONEY
I said I wished it was clear so that we could go get a drink.

PHONEY 2
Well we're in no condition to deliver anything now.

MOLLY
That has to be them.

JAKE
Hey you guys.

PHONEY
That's us.

JAKE
The last guy that tipped you, I need to see that dollar he gave you.

PHONEY
No way. We worked hard for that dollar.

MOLLY
He doesn't want to take it. He just needs to see it.

(Phoney 2 pulls Phoney aside)

PHONEY 2
Hey, we should make them make our delivery for us.

PHONEY
How are we going to do that?

PHONEY 2
Tell him you'll let him see the dollar after they make the delivery for us.

PHONEY
Hey, yeah.

(The turn back to Jake and Molly.)

PHONEY
What's so important about this dollar?

JAKE
I wrote an idea on it.

PHONEY
This is a pretty important idea?

JAKE
Very.

PHONEY
And we'd be helping you out by letting you see this dollar?

JAKE

Yes.

PHONEY

Okay, so you help us out and we help you out.

MOLLY

What do you mean?

PHONEY 2

We have to make one more delivery tonight, but seem to have found ourselves in no condition to make that delivery. All you got to do is take our truck and make one delivery, come back here and we'll let you see that dollar.

JAKE

Fine.

MOLLY

Jake, this is ridiculous. Just let him see the dollar.

PHONEY

If that's the way you feel about it them maybe-

JAKE

Look I said I'd do it. I don't have time to argue about it. Where are the keys?

(Phoney hands over the keys.)

PHONEY

2675 Newberry Street, have fun.

(The Phoney's exit.)

MOLLY

Newberry Street, no.

JAKE

What?

                              MOLLY
That's ridiculous. It will take close to an hour
just to get out there.

                              JAKE
That long?

                              MOLLY
Yeah. Rich people like to live out from the dreary
lives of us regular folks.

                              JAKE
Speaking of folks, what about your dad?

                              MOLLY
With all this I almost forgot about him. I need to
check on him. Can you please...?

                              JAKE
It's only a little out of the way. Let's go.

                    (They exit. End of scene one)

Act II

Scene 2

(Jake and Molly are driving in the delivery truck. Molly has a notebook.)

JAKE
Are you sure about this? Maybe you should stay with your dad.

MOLLY
Dad's fine. I asked Mrs. Shelby to keep an eye on him while we were gone.

JAKE
What's with the notebook?

MOLLY
It's why I'm coming with you. You can be coming up with ideas while we drive. Maybe you'll remember what you wrote earlier.

JAKE
Great idea.

MOLLY
Have you had any ideas yet?

JAKE
Well, I was thinking about... no, that's stupid.

MOLLY
What's stupid? Anything is better than nothing at this point, right?

JAKE
I was thinking about Satan, since I'm having a hellish day.

MOLLY
Okay.

                    JAKE
What would happen if Satan went to God and said he was sorry? What if Satan repented?

                    MOLLY
Okay, we have that down. Where does it go from there?

                    JAKE
I haven't a clue? If only I had more time.

                    MOLLY
Well, we could always just sign for the delivery and pretend we did the job.

                    JAKE
We can't do that; those guys could lose their jobs.

                    MOLLY
And serves them right for making you go through this.

                    JAKE
Let's just get back to the brainstorming.

                    MOLLY
Maybe we're trying to go too broad. Don't some writers start with a character and see where the story goes.

                    JAKE
Some.

                    MOLLY
Okay, so we need a character.

                    JAKE
I hate coming up with names. They never fit. I usually grab one from something that's close at hand at the time.

                    MOLLY
There are plenty of names on the roster. Like this guy we are delivering too, a Mr. Miller. There's got to be a story behind that name.

                    JAKE
Miller, Miller. He could be a carpenter, a
business man.

                    MOLLY
An astronaut, a secret agent, a hitman.

                    JAKE
A hitman?

                    MOLLY
Well, aren't you looking for a killer idea?

                    JAKE
Yes. You ought to be ashamed by the way.

                    MOLLY
What?

                    JAKE
Hitman, killer idea.

                    MOLLY
I didn't mean that. I just meant don't you need
something big, fantastic.

                    JAKE
Something that will knock them dead.

                    MOLLY
Ha ha.

                    JAKE
I do, but that doesn't mean the character has to
be completely out of the ordinary. At least not
starting out. There have been great books and
movies written about ordinary cops, scientists,
IRS agents.

                    MOLLY
IRS agents?

JAKE
Stranger than Fiction. Anyway, the point is that it's not just the character, it's the situation. Like you and your dad... do mind if I ask what that situation is?

MOLLY
Dad was in an accident several years ago. Broke his back and lost the use of his legs.

JAKE
Now you're taking care of him.

MOLLY
Yep.

JAKE
Alone? I have never seen anyone else around.

MOLLY
Yeah, alone. My sister lives in Iowa. My mother, she skipped out years ago and hasn't been back since. What about you. What's your situation? You seem to have about as lively of a social life as I do.

JAKE
Not much motivation to. I'm the quintessential starving artist. Working a dead end job to pay rent and eat while desperately trying to get published. Not the greatest way to start a relationship. So I'll get invited to a party now and then, but if I go I feel guilty because I should be working on my writing and if I don't go I can't write because I'm thinking about what I could be missing. Hey, what's the address for the delivery? 2675 Newberry Street?

MOLLY
Yeah.

JAKE
Great, we're here. Let's get this done.

(They exit. End of scene two)

Act II

Scene 3

(Molly and Jake are back in the truck.)

MOLLY
Whew, that was...

JAKE
Yeah.

MOLLY
Who puts a big screen television on the fourth floor of their house?

JAKE
Who in the world has a four story house just for themselves?

MOLLY
How about that? Is that worth going in the notebook for an idea?

JAKE
It has potential. A four story house might make for a great bottle.

MOLLY
A bottle.

JAKE
It's when you have a story take place for the most part in a very contained area.

MOLLY
So it would be a big bottle.

JAKE
Exactly. Plenty of places that the characters could separate themselves to have all their different interactions.

                        MOLLY
So we have Mr. Miller, by day a plumber, by
night...

                        JAKE
Still a plumber, who gets called to a four story
house where there is a dinner party going on but,
something is wrong with the pipes. While he is
there someone is murdered.

                        MOLLY
Murdered with one of his tools.

                        JAKE
It will later be revealed that he was called by
the murderer to be there to take the fall for the
killing.

                        MOLLY
And it just so happens that he is more involved in
the whole plot than the reader is led to believe.

                        JAKE
Now you're getting it. Okay so.

                (They pass a woman walking hunched
                over along the side of the road.)

                        JAKE
What was that?

                        MOLLY
It looked like someone in pain. Look, there's a
car pulled over, it's empty. Maybe it was her car.

                        JAKE
Hold on.

                (He cranks the wheel and they
                drive back to the woman.)

                        JAKE
Ma'am, ma'am are you okay.

CONNIE
Oh thank God, thank God. My car broke down and I left the house in such a aaaaggghhh, rush that I forget to take my cell phone and unnnngggh!

JAKE
What's the matter?

CONNIE
I need to call an ambulance. I think I'm going into labor.

>   (Jake pulls off his jacket and wraps it around her shoulders. He helps her into the truck.)

JAKE
Okay, just remain calm. We'll get you there as soon as we can.

CONNIE
I'll be fine, if you could just call-

JAKE
I don't have a cell phone.

MOLLY
Me either.

CONNIE
You're kidding.

JAKE & MOLLY
Can't afford it.

CONNIE
Well then, to the hospital Benson.

>   (Pantomime wild driving. Stop. Jake and Molly help Connie out.)

MOLLY
We're here. Let's get you inside.

>   (They are helping Connie to exit when two police officers enter.)

                    OFFICER 1
Freeze.

                    OFFICER 2
Put your hands in the air.

                    JAKE
We'll drop her.

                    CONNIE
Eaaaaggghh!

                    OFFICER 1
They're hurting her.

                    MOLLY
No we're-

          (The officers rush them. Officer 1
          restrains Molly easily, Officer 2
          tackles Jake. Connie starts
          kicking the Officer 2.)

                    CONNIE
Get off him you moron. He's helping me. I'm preg... aiiiee! I'm giving birth!

          (Lights out. End of scene three)

Act III

Scene 1

(Jake and Molly are outside with the police officers.)

OFFICER 1
You realize that we should be giving you a ticket for speeding.

OFFICER 2
Reckless endangerment.

OFFICER 1
Resisting arrest.

MOLLY
Resisting arrest. Your partner tackled Jake. All he did was try to keep from having his face smashed into the road.

OFFICER 2
We don't need to get caught up in the details. The point is, under the circumstances, we are going to let you off with a warning.

JAKE
Thank you officer.

OFFICER 1
You two have a good night now, and drive safe.

(The officers exit.)

MOLLY
Why that... how can you just thank him like that? Why do you let people walk all over you like that?

JAKE
What?

MOLLY
Milton, the delivery guys, those officers. You didn't argue at all, just caved in to what they wanted.

JAKE
Because. What good would arguing do? The cops weren't going to give us a ticket so no harm, no foul. Had I argued simply to prove that I was not in the wrong they may have noticed that we aren't actually employees of this delivery company and that could get us in a lot more trouble. Now I can get back and get my dollar.

MOLLY
Your dollar, I completely forgot about it. Let's go.

(They exit. End of scene one)

Act III

Scene 2

(The Phoney's are sitting outside the bar.)

PHONEY
So I told her that my Lamborghini is in the shop. Well, it is. It's in the shop 'cause I haven't bought it yet.

(Jake and Molly enter.)

PHONEY 2
'S about time. Bar closed hour and a half ago. Where you been.

JAKE
It's a long story.

MOLLY
We made the delivery, now where's his dollar.

PHONEY
Dollar?

JAKE
The dollar that you were going to give me for making the delivery for you.

PHONEY
Oh that dollar, had the girl's phone number on it, right?

MOLLY
No, the dollar that had a bunch of writing on it.

PHONEY 2
I remember. See, I tol' you we weren't supposed to spend that.

JAKE
You spent it?

                    PHONEY 2
Lost it is more like it.

                    PHONEY
I don't know what happened. I watched the guy. I knew where the queen was.

                    MOLLY
The queen?

                    PHONEY
There were only three cards. I was going to double my money. Others were doing it.

                    JAKE
You got grifted. How could you do that? Everybody knows that three card monte is a con.

                    PHONEY
Other people were winning.

                    JAKE
Those other people were working with the dealer.

                        (Jake throws his hands in the air
                        and sits down on the curb bowing
                        his head dejectedly. Molly smacks
                        and berates the Phoneys offstage
                        then sits next to Jake.)

                    JAKE
Well that's it. The idea is gone.

                    MOLLY
You can't give up yet.

                        (She pulls him up by the arm. He
                        stumbles into her and they steady
                        each other. There is a tense
                        moment.)

                    MOLLY
We can still get your dollar back. This con can't have gone very far.

                        (They exit. End of scene two.)

Act III

Scene 3

(A group is gathered around Con's cardboard box/table. He is running a three card monte con. Molly and Jake enter opposite.)

JAKE
There he is.

MOLLY
They can't be making that much money at this time of night.

JAKE
Who knows? Maybe they are just practicing, making sure they have their con in order.

MOLLY
Okay, let's go get your dollar back.

JAKE
How? We can't win?

MOLLY
We've still got the tip Mr. Miller gave us.

JAKE
So.

MOLLY
What con man wouldn't trade a twenty for a one?

JAKE
He might think that we are trying to con him.

MOLLY
Excuse me. Excuse me, gentlemen. Can I have your attention?

(All the guys turn to look at Molly.)

                    MOLLY
Thank you. I was told by an acquaintance that they
lost some money to you.

                    CON
Lady, I don't give refunds.

                    MOLLY
I don't expect you to. I'm sure you won the money
fair and square. And it's yours but I was hoping
that I could buy one of the dollars back from you.

                    CON
You want to buy one of the dollars back?

                    MOLLY
Yes. My friend wrote something down on the dollar
and he needs to have it back for a meeting
tomorrow. I'm willing to pay twenty dollars for
it. That's not a bad profit, wouldn't you say.

                    SHILL
What's it got on it?

                    MOLLY
A bunch of writing, an idea.

                    CON
I don't look much at money past the numbers up in
the corner. Somebody might have won it off me.

                    MOLLY
I doubt that.

                    CON
All right boys, check your pockets.

            (The Shill takes out a dollar and
            scribbles on it.)

                    SHILL
I think I got it.

            (He holds it out for Molly to take
            it. Just before she can get it, it

"slips out of her hand and the wind takes it away.)

JAKE

Hey.

SHILL

Oops.

MOLLY

Get it!

(Jake runs after the dollar, exits. Molly starts after it.)

SHILL

Where's my twenty?

(Molly runs back, hands him the twenty, and exits.)

CON

What'd his dollar say?

SHILL

His, who knows. I wrote, "You should listen to P.T. Barnum."

CON

That's rich. Let's get out of here boys.

(The group exits. End of scene three.)

Act IV

Scene 1

(A bridge. The dollar flutters along the edge. There is a worker underneath in the supports of the bridge. Jake and Molly enter.)

MOLLY

There it is.

(The worker's safety rope falls away and he clutches at the support.)

FRANK

Help!

JAKE

What was that?

(Jake and molly run to the edge of the bridge. They spot the worker.)

FRANK

Help me!

MOLLY

He's going to fall.

(Jake takes one panicked look at the dollar. He takes off his belt and hands one end to Molly.)

JAKE

Hold this.

(Jake holds the other end and leans out to the worker.)

JAKE

Take my hand.

(The worker takes his hand and with much effort Jake and Molly

                    haul him up to safety. They all
                    collapse to the ground.)

                         FRANK
Thankyouthankyouthankyou, thank you. How can I
ever repay you?

                         JAKE
It's okay.

                         MOLLY
Jake, the dollar.

                    (Jake looks to where the dollar
                    was just in time to see if flutter
                    over the side and be lost to
                    darkness.)

                         JAKE & MOLLY
No!

                         FRANK
What?

                         JAKE
It's gone.

                         FRANK
What's gone?

                         MOLLY
The dollar.

                         FRANK
A dollar. I'll gladly pay you-

                         JAKE
Oh what's the use?

                    (Jake hangs his head and walks
                    off.)

                         FRANK
Hey, what's you name, I... What's the matter?

MOLLY
He has been chasing that dollar all night.

FRANK
A special dollar.

MOLLY
Very. It had his masterpiece idea on it.

FRANK
And you lost it because you were saving me. Is there anything I can do?

MOLLY
Just... be more careful next time.

>   (She exits after Jake. End of scene one.)

Act IV

Scene 2

(Jake walks along the city streets alone. Molly enters and catches up to him. She takes his arm.)

MOLLY
So what now?

JAKE
It's over Molly. You should go home and get some rest.

MOLLY
It's not over. We've still got some time.

JAKE
You still think I can come up with a better idea that will impress Mr. Jenkins?

MOLLY
You don't think you can?

JAKE
I have nothing. All I can think about is the fact that I have nothing and I have to walk into that meeting with nothing.

MOLLY
So you're just going to give up? You're not even going to try.

JAKE
Well, it's not like it's the end of the world. There are other publishers. Maybe one of them will like my idea, or I'll come up with a new one that is better in a day or a week. For tonight, or this morning, as it were, I am done writing.

MOLLY
Okay then. There's no point dwelling. I want you to come with me.

JAKE
Where?

MOLLY
I know a rooftop where the sunrise over the city is, for lack of a better word, inspiring. Let's just go enjoy.

(They climb up a ladder to a roof.)

JAKE
Wow, this place is neat. How did you find it?

MOLLY
Back when I was going to school. I took an art class and we had to do some cityscapes and stuff like that. I scoured the city for the right spot. I used to come here to paint all the time. Even if I was painting a dragon or a river, I did it here. There's just something about this spot.

(The sun rises tinting the rooftop with shades of orange and red. Jake and Molly Gaze out at the sunset and steal looks at each other. Jake sighs.)

JAKE
Well, it's about time for me to go face the music.

(They share an are-they-gonna-kiss moment before Jake breaks away and climbs down off the roof. He climbs partway down and stops.)

JAKE
Thanks for everything. It's been...

MOLLY
The writer, at a loss for words. Cute.

JAKE
Bye.

(He exits.)

MOLLY
Bye.
(pause)
I wish I had the colors to paint this night. What a night... yeah, what a night. Oh. Jake, that's it.

> (She climbs down and exits at a run after Jake. End of scene two.)

Act IV

Scene 3

(The Tabularasa publishing offices just as at the beginning. Cilia knocks on Mr. Jenkins' door.

GARFORD

Yes.

CILIA

Your nine o'clock is here.

GARFORD

Ah, the young man. Bring him in.

(Jake enters.)

GARFORD

Have a seat.

JAKE

No thanks. I'll stand. This will be quick anyway. I just came to apologize for wasting your time and say that.

MOLLY

(Off stage)
Jake! Jake!

(Molly enters and crowds into the office.)

GARFORD

Who is this, what's going on?

JAKE

Molly, what are you-

MOLLY

Your idea, you have it.

JAKE

No, I don't.

MOLLY
Yes, you do.

CILIA
Excuse us ma'am, but you are interrupting an important meeting.

MOLLY
Tell them about your night.

JAKE
Why?

MOLLY
Tell them about it from start to finish.

>(Everyone turns to see what Jake will do.)

JAKE
Okay. It started as I left your offices last night. I was so shocked that you hadn't liked my idea that I left my notebook in your office. It had other ideas that I'd written down just in case...

>(Jake stops talking and pantomimes telling more of the story. Cilia and Garford sit down to listen.)

JAKE
And I owe him three dollars today. I took his money and...

>(More pantomime.)

JAKE
Headed out for the delivery-

MOLLY
Taking the time to take me to check on my father.

>(Pantomime)

                    JAKE
Arrived at the hospital, I guess that's where my
jacket is.

          (Pantomime more.)

                    JAKE
Dollar was blown off the side of the bridge.

                    MOLLY
He didn't just miss it. He stopped to save
someone's life.

                    JAKE
So I gave up. We watched the sun rise from the
rooftops and then I came here.

          (Garford contemplates while
          everyone waits on edge.)

                    GARFORD
I have to be honest with you. I can't choose
between that and your first story. They are both
brilliant.

                    JAKE
But I thought you said...

                    GARFORD
I do that to every author when I intend to publish
their work. If they are going to work for me they
have to be willing to face two things. First that
what they think is great isn't always so and they
have to be able to let it go and work on something
else. Second, they have to be able to face the
potential of the worst writer's block of their
lives. Every writer has something that helps them
out of it, and it looks to me like you've found
it. Looks like you'll be publishing two books with
us for starters.

                    CILIA
Of course your night could use a little work. I
just don't quite like the ending.

                    GARFORD
It does need something.

                     MOLLY
How about this?

            (Molly takes Jakes face in her
            hands and kisses him to blackout.)

The Rough Stuff

I don't mean rough as in rough drafts. Several of the pieces that are in this compilation are little more than the original rough drafts. By rough I mean the stuff that was hard to write.
As we were preparing for the wedding I had to borrow Rolodex cards from the coordinator to rewrite my speech. I was moving things around, adding new and cutting old.

Wedding Speech

In a world such as ours, a world so large, fast-paced, and at times dark and foreboding, what a treasure it is to walk it with another.
Arden, if anyone tells you that you are lucky to have Ryan just smile and nod and know that he is lucky to have you. He is lucky to have a beautiful, smart woman who lightens his heart and completes him.
Ryan, if anyone tells you that you are lucky to have Arden just smile and nod and know that she is lucky to have you. She is lucky to have a patient, loving, God fearing man such as you.
There will be times when you will want her to take life more seriously and you will be right. There will be times when she will want you to lighten up and she will be right. You will carry her when she is weak, and she will lift you up when all you want to do is fall. You will wipe her tears away and she will hold you and help you cry. You will smile when she enters the room, and she will treasure these moments as they come.
You are more than lucky to have each other. You are blessed. And, as long as you both follow the One who created you for each other and brought you together, you will be blessed. Ryan, I love you cuz, Arden, welcome to the family. May your life be filled with love.

My father had always wanted to use the book of Ecclesiastes to do a funeral, though he never was able to. When it came time for his funeral I tried to do what I thought he would. I had tried to write the service many times over the week, but found myself, much like my father, scribbling this out on a piece of paper at midnight the night before. I even ended up sticking in the intro as the thought struck me up in front of everyone.

My Father's Funeral

My father always wanted to do a funeral from the book of Ecclesiastes and I think I finally know why. It's because it shows us what it all amounts to, where we stand in the whole scheme of things and in relation to God.

Ecclesiastes Ch 11
Cast your bread on the surface of the waters, for you will find it after many days.
Divide your portion to seven, or even to eight, for you do not know what misfortune may occur on the earth.
If the clouds are full, they pour out rain upon the earth; and whether a tree falls toward the south or toward the north, wherever the tree falls, there it lies.
He who watches the wind will not sow and he who looks at the clouds will not reap.
Just as you do not know the path of the wind and how bones are formed in the womb of the pregnant woman, so you do not know the activity of God who makes all things.
Sow your seed in the morning and do not be idle in the evening, for you do not know whether morning or evening sowing will succeed, or whether both of them alike will be good.
The light is pleasant, and it is good for the eyes to see the sun.
Indeed, if a man should live many years, let him rejoice in them all, and let him remember the days of darkness, for they will be many.
Everything that is to come will be futility.
Rejoice, young man, during your childhood, and let your heart be pleasant during the days of

young manhood. And follow the impulses of your heart and the desires of your eyes yet know that God will bring you to judgment for all these things.

So, remove grief and anger from your heart and put away pain from your body, because childhood and the prime of life are fleeting.

For 19 years this was what my father feared. Death. The fun and games would end and he would come face to face with a creator who would ask, "Bob, I knocked, why didn't you open the door? I called out to you, why did you ignore my voice?"

Despite daily Bible reading and parents that were living examples, Bob McCone was still living for Bob Mc Cone. Every night he would go to bed praying for forgiveness just in case that night was his last. Waking the next day, he went on living life his own way.

One day while walking across the Long Beach State campus he had a conversation with God. He would often relate it to people he was trying to reach. It went like this:

God, I know you are real and this is ridiculous. Either I tell you to go to Hell, and I'll live my own way for seventy years and then I will, or I let you have me, all of me.

He let God have him and no longer feared this day. The next day he woke and faced the same decision, do I let God control me today, or do I take control back.

For the next forty-three years he faced that decision every day. It was that daily submission to God that made my father who he was, the man we loved. It made him able to love when others couldn't or wouldn't. It made him able to forgive time and time again, seventy times seven and beyond. It gave him a tender heart that ached for all those around him. We loved him for all these things, his heart that went out to us, his time he gave to us, the patience he had with us, the peace he brought to us.

It was this daily choice that made my father into a man who touched lives, leaving them always for the better.

Ecclesiastes Ch 12

Remember also your Creator in the days of your youth, before the evil days come and the years draw near when you will say, "I have no delight in them"; before the sun and the light, the moon and the stars are darkened, and clouds return after the rain; in the day that the watchmen of the house tremble, and mighty men stoop, the grinding ones stand idle because they are few, and those who look through windows grow dim; and the doors on the street are shut as the sound of the grinding mill is low, and one will arise at the sound of the bird, and all the daughters of song will sing softly.

Furthermore, men are afraid of a high place and of terrors on the road; the almond tree blossoms, the grasshopper drags himself along, and the caperberry is ineffective. For man goes to his eternal home while mourners go about in the street.

Remember Him before the silver cord is broken and the golden bowl is crushed, the pitcher by the well is shattered and the wheel at the cistern is crushed; then the dust will return to the earth as it was, and the spirit will return to God who gave it.

"Vanity of vanities," says the Preacher, "all is vanity!"

In addition to being a wise man, the Preacher also taught the people knowledge; and he pondered, searched out and arranged many proverbs.

The Preacher sought to find delightful words and to write words of truth correctly.

The words of wise men are like goads, and masters of these collections are like well-driven nails; they are given by one Shepherd.

But beyond this, my son, be warned: the writing of many books is endless, and excessive devotion to books is wearying to the body.

The conclusion, when all has been heard, is: fear God and keep His commandments, because this applies to every person.

For God will bring every act to judgment, everything which is hidden, whether it is good or evil.

Jesus explained the commandments of God as: Love God with all you heart, soul, and mind, and love your neighbor as yourself. My father did this. Were he speaking to you today he would not bother with this doctrine or that, he would plead with us to love God and love others, all others. It's all that really matters. Love covers a multitude of sins and when we love, we will touch others' lives – as my father did – leaving them <u>always</u> for the better.

Lines or sections that I happened to like from other projects.

Bits and Pieces

In a world where planes, trains, and cars traverse the skyways and byways I walk in the in-betweens. I am a wizard in this realm of what is and what might be.
-cover letter I started to write

I've done a lot of stupid things in my life. In each of them there was one thing that ran constant, besides me being an idiot. Through all of them I knew that I could possibly get severely hurt so I was going, dontletthishurt-dontletthishurt. Each time I ended up coming out cut, scraped, burned, or generally banged up, usually in a bunch of pain, but other than that I was more or less undamaged. Nothing a little ice, an ace bandage, and a day taking it easy couldn't handle. This time it was different.
-writing about tearing my spleen in half

It began with a prophecy made by a false prophet. Yet those words, so simple to speak would set nations against each other and force a young man to abandon everything he knew to try and bring peace back to his world.
-NaNoWriMo project

During junior high and high school I read like Exxon spilled oil.

Do not fear the draft. It is a good thing. So you write something and it doesn't go perfectly from your brain to keyboard to paper. That does not mean that you are not a good writer. You are a writer, good, bad, or otherwise.

I am not one of those writers who let's the characters take the story where they want it to

go. I am an iron-fisted dictator who hammers my stories together the way I want them
-excerpts from my book on writing

"I'm afraid your eyes are brown. There may have been a hint of green, but it was definitely not vampire-story-eyes green."
"Are you sure?" Brody asked.
"Go look in the entryway mirror," Wickman said.
"Vampires can't see themselves in the mirror."
"Then that gives us more proof that you are not a vampire. I saw you in the mirror on the way in."
"Of course *you* saw me in the mirror," Brody said. "You can see me in the mirror, but I can't see me in the mirror. It would be too easy for people to discover vampires if they couldn't see them in a mirror."
"Oh," Wickman said.
"Boys, would you set the table," Wickman's mom called.
-Irreverent Towards Vampires

LOU
Guys, this isn't going to happen.

AL
It has to. We have to raise bail money.

MANNY
They've already paid for a show. We do it and then go bail out the actors.

LOU
I get the plan, but guys, it's the Bible in Shorts, which, aside from being completely irreverent, is a play that encompasses thousands of years, huge battles, and the relocation of an entire nation. How are three guys going to pull that off?

MANNY
Props. We have loads of props. They're like explosions in an action movie, they take care of everything.
-The Bible In Shorts

"I have no problem with believing something because you want to, but I have a big problem with saying that something is true so that you feel better about believing it."
-end to my Book of Questions

When do you step back and allow life to run its course without trying to grasp the reins? Those horses are perfectly capable of running smoothly without your intervention. Sure they might not go the direction you want, but even with you fighting them they still may not.
-writing about dad's cancer